This Workbook Belongs to:

Additional recommended workbooks for future 2nd graders:

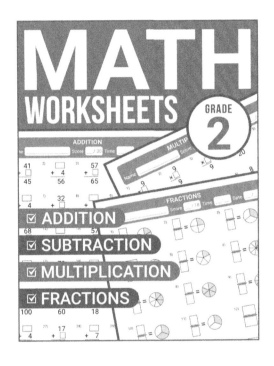

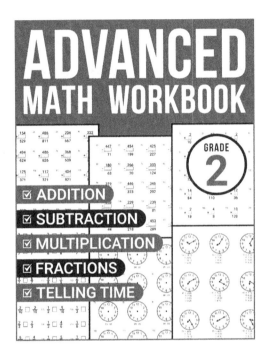

www.nermilio.com

Table of Contents

Addition

Add 2-digit and 1-digit numbers in columns and write the correct answer!

1)
```
   92
+   2
```

2)
```
   96
+   9
```

3)
```
   50
+   1
```

4)
```
   27
+   6
```

5)
```
    2
+  22
```

6)
```
    3
+  46
```

7)
```
    7
+  17
```

8)
```
   82
+   3
```

9)
```
    5
+  50
```

10)
```
   49
+   9
```

11)
```
    5
+  59
```

12)
```
   87
+   4
```

13)
```
   60
+   7
```

14)
```
    9
+  31
```

15)
```
    5
+  68
```

16)
```
   72
+   7
```

17)
```
    7
+  99
```

18)
```
    3
+  20
```

19)
```
    3
+  81
```

20)
```
    5
+  51
```

21)
```
   39
+   8
```

22)
```
    7
+  62
```

23)
```
    8
+  95
```

24)
```
   60
+   9
```

25)
```
   94
+   9
```

26)
```
    2
+  53
```

27)
```
   26
+   1
```

28)
```
   73
+   4
```

29)
```
   55
+   4
```

30)
```
    1
+  27
```

1)   6
 + 96

2)   6
 + 69

3)   1
 + 11

4)   8
 + 92

5)   5
 + 25

6)   2
 + 82

7)   6
 + 17

8)   25
 + 3

9)   64
 + 6

10) 11
 + 4

11)   8
 + 75

12)   9
 + 92

13) 51
 + 2

14)   5
 + 76

15)   1
 + 42

16)   5
 + 91

17)   5
 + 81

18) 20
 + 5

19) 68
 + 2

20) 83
 + 6

21)   9
 + 15

22)   2
 + 26

23) 26
 + 9

24)   7
 + 99

25)   6
 + 16

26) 33
 + 1

27) 97
 + 6

28) 85
 + 3

29)   9
 + 73

30) 65
 + 1

1)   77
   + 3

2)   1
   + 28

3)   24
   + 5

4)   54
   + 9

5)   54
   + 9

6)   6
   + 98

7)   4
   + 66

8)   73
   + 4

9)   93
   + 2

10)   77
   + 6

11)   4
   + 17

12)   6
   + 15

13)   26
   + 1

14)   59
   + 4

15)   5
   + 92

16)   95
   + 7

17)   32
   + 3

18)   8
   + 42

19)   9
   + 39

20)   7
   + 32

21)   54
   + 1

22)   47
   + 4

23)   60
   + 4

24)   2
   + 16

25)   12
   + 6

26)   4
   + 55

27)   88
   + 4

28)   90
   + 3

29)   19
   + 9

30)   8
   + 46

1)   9
  + 96

2)   32
  + 6

3)   37
  + 6

4)   21
  + 8

5)   4
  + 17

6)   4
  + 40

7)   35
  + 7

8)   20
  + 8

9)   4
  + 36

10)   74
  + 1

11)   57
  + 6

12)   8
  + 51

13)   40
  + 1

14)   6
  + 60

15)   8
  + 32

16)   77
  + 2

17)   14
  + 1

18)   40
  + 5

19)   35
  + 2

20)   1
  + 35

21)   9
  + 51

22)   18
  + 4

23)   22
  + 8

24)   87
  + 3

25)   9
  + 25

26)   42
  + 7

27)   77
  + 4

28)   8
  + 87

29)   4
  + 86

30)   40
  + 2

1) 8 + 18

2) 33 + 3

3) 71 + 2

4) 9 + 24

5) 12 + 3

6) 2 + 36

7) 7 + 78

8) 7 + 72

9) 1 + 90

10) 84 + 6

11) 3 + 85

12) 60 + 9

13) 15 + 2

14) 73 + 5

15) 10 + 1

16) 7 + 49

17) 83 + 5

18) 4 + 67

19) 9 + 75

20) 9 + 60

21) 3 + 30

22) 1 + 44

23) 81 + 3

24) 7 + 80

25) 8 + 86

26) 69 + 8

27) 71 + 7

28) 17 + 1

29) 8 + 69

30) 4 + 44

1) 81
   + 5

2) 17
   + 7

3) 85
   + 8

4)   3
   + 79

5) 67
   + 2

6) 93
   + 2

7)   2
   + 41

8)   3
   + 33

9)   4
   + 86

10)   3
    + 32

11) 68
    + 4

12) 24
    + 8

13) 45
    + 3

14) 55
    + 3

15) 48
    + 2

16)   3
    + 42

17) 51
    + 7

18) 19
    + 8

19)   4
    + 55

20) 25
    + 8

21) 30
    + 9

22)   3
    + 70

23)   7
    + 67

24) 64
    + 4

25)   9
    + 93

26)   7
    + 89

27) 98
    + 9

28) 42
    + 1

29)   9
    + 14

30)   2
    + 17

1)
$$41 + 1$$

2)
$$5 + 49$$

3)
$$8 + 39$$

4)
$$80 + 5$$

5)
$$4 + 90$$

6)
$$3 + 18$$

7)
$$12 + 5$$

8)
$$8 + 99$$

9)
$$25 + 7$$

10)
$$5 + 22$$

11)
$$15 + 8$$

12)
$$83 + 5$$

13)
$$2 + 68$$

14)
$$17 + 3$$

15)
$$51 + 5$$

16)
$$4 + 77$$

17)
$$8 + 63$$

18)
$$5 + 37$$

19)
$$7 + 29$$

20)
$$7 + 91$$

21)
$$6 + 68$$

22)
$$1 + 62$$

23)
$$83 + 7$$

24)
$$7 + 35$$

25)
$$45 + 3$$

26)
$$8 + 41$$

27)
$$5 + 22$$

28)
$$41 + 9$$

29)
$$38 + 2$$

30)
$$65 + 4$$

1)
$$
\begin{array}{r}
21 \\
+\ 4 \\
\hline
\end{array}
$$

2)
$$
\begin{array}{r}
31 \\
+\ 7 \\
\hline
\end{array}
$$

3)
$$
\begin{array}{r}
7 \\
+\ 47 \\
\hline
\end{array}
$$

4)
$$
\begin{array}{r}
65 \\
+\ 6 \\
\hline
\end{array}
$$

5)
$$
\begin{array}{r}
2 \\
+\ 93 \\
\hline
\end{array}
$$

6)
$$
\begin{array}{r}
6 \\
+\ 43 \\
\hline
\end{array}
$$

7)
$$
\begin{array}{r}
26 \\
+\ 8 \\
\hline
\end{array}
$$

8)
$$
\begin{array}{r}
9 \\
+\ 44 \\
\hline
\end{array}
$$

9)
$$
\begin{array}{r}
22 \\
+\ 2 \\
\hline
\end{array}
$$

10)
$$
\begin{array}{r}
42 \\
+\ 1 \\
\hline
\end{array}
$$

11)
$$
\begin{array}{r}
53 \\
+\ 9 \\
\hline
\end{array}
$$

12)
$$
\begin{array}{r}
4 \\
+\ 13 \\
\hline
\end{array}
$$

13)
$$
\begin{array}{r}
97 \\
+\ 6 \\
\hline
\end{array}
$$

14)
$$
\begin{array}{r}
39 \\
+\ 3 \\
\hline
\end{array}
$$

15)
$$
\begin{array}{r}
69 \\
+\ 5 \\
\hline
\end{array}
$$

16)
$$
\begin{array}{r}
50 \\
+\ 5 \\
\hline
\end{array}
$$

17)
$$
\begin{array}{r}
9 \\
+\ 74 \\
\hline
\end{array}
$$

18)
$$
\begin{array}{r}
7 \\
+\ 96 \\
\hline
\end{array}
$$

19)
$$
\begin{array}{r}
25 \\
+\ 6 \\
\hline
\end{array}
$$

20)
$$
\begin{array}{r}
68 \\
+\ 1 \\
\hline
\end{array}
$$

21)
$$
\begin{array}{r}
60 \\
+\ 6 \\
\hline
\end{array}
$$

22)
$$
\begin{array}{r}
8 \\
+\ 43 \\
\hline
\end{array}
$$

23)
$$
\begin{array}{r}
59 \\
+\ 9 \\
\hline
\end{array}
$$

24)
$$
\begin{array}{r}
3 \\
+\ 22 \\
\hline
\end{array}
$$

25)
$$
\begin{array}{r}
73 \\
+\ 3 \\
\hline
\end{array}
$$

26)
$$
\begin{array}{r}
9 \\
+\ 96 \\
\hline
\end{array}
$$

27)
$$
\begin{array}{r}
18 \\
+\ 1 \\
\hline
\end{array}
$$

28)
$$
\begin{array}{r}
40 \\
+\ 6 \\
\hline
\end{array}
$$

29)
$$
\begin{array}{r}
88 \\
+\ 5 \\
\hline
\end{array}
$$

30)
$$
\begin{array}{r}
88 \\
+\ 9 \\
\hline
\end{array}
$$

Addition

1) 13
  + 49

2) 77
  + 19

3) 95
  + 61

4) 71
  + 89

5) 64
  + 18

6) 54
  + 77

7) 36
  + 69

8) 52
  + 38

9) 86
  + 92

10) 16
  + 65

11) 65
  + 76

12) 27
  + 61

13) 75
  + 50

14) 82
  + 98

15) 71
  + 84

16) 14
  + 71

17) 45
  + 19

18) 48
  + 36

19) 32
  + 92

20) 31
  + 95

21) 90
  + 26

22) 13
  + 70

23) 23
  + 92

24) 46
  + 99

25) 58
  + 17

26) 38
  + 95

27) 78
  + 73

28) 69
  + 28

29) 45
  + 76

30) 86
  + 25

1) 38 + 75

2) 10 + 96

3) 25 + 62

4) 52 + 25

5) 55 + 48

6) 40 + 36

7) 18 + 54

8) 54 + 44

9) 71 + 41

10) 62 + 90

11) 26 + 39

12) 42 + 11

13) 29 + 45

14) 11 + 49

15) 19 + 22

16) 85 + 58

17) 15 + 22

18) 54 + 84

19) 84 + 69

20) 54 + 34

21) 29 + 98

22) 26 + 93

23) 38 + 67

24) 41 + 44

25) 59 + 93

26) 61 + 26

27) 99 + 76

28) 98 + 93

29) 59 + 30

30) 56 + 48

1) 26 + 19

2) 99 + 22

3) 84 + 42

4) 21 + 69

5) 85 + 83

6) 70 + 89

7) 22 + 32

8) 46 + 19

9) 63 + 80

10) 68 + 78

11) 86 + 55

12) 31 + 82

13) 92 + 12

14) 18 + 63

15) 70 + 58

16) 92 + 55

17) 17 + 38

18) 87 + 86

19) 96 + 45

20) 46 + 70

21) 44 + 94

22) 38 + 56

23) 37 + 60

24) 50 + 73

25) 20 + 87

26) 64 + 42

27) 47 + 22

28) 18 + 57

29) 87 + 11

30) 82 + 50

1)
$$77 + 70$$

2)
$$12 + 78$$

3)
$$54 + 89$$

4)
$$97 + 44$$

5)
$$55 + 84$$

6)
$$37 + 64$$

7)
$$27 + 31$$

8)
$$99 + 93$$

9)
$$27 + 19$$

10)
$$92 + 14$$

11)
$$29 + 18$$

12)
$$74 + 46$$

13)
$$93 + 70$$

14)
$$46 + 44$$

15)
$$77 + 49$$

16)
$$33 + 35$$

17)
$$30 + 11$$

18)
$$55 + 63$$

19)
$$58 + 40$$

20)
$$52 + 88$$

21)
$$87 + 84$$

22)
$$67 + 57$$

23)
$$70 + 54$$

24)
$$99 + 57$$

25)
$$55 + 70$$

26)
$$59 + 29$$

27)
$$80 + 47$$

28)
$$10 + 57$$

29)
$$80 + 85$$

30)
$$64 + 63$$

1)
$$\begin{array}{r} 14 \\ + 68 \\ \hline \end{array}$$

2)
$$\begin{array}{r} 53 \\ + 49 \\ \hline \end{array}$$

3)
$$\begin{array}{r} 80 \\ + 94 \\ \hline \end{array}$$

4)
$$\begin{array}{r} 51 \\ + 64 \\ \hline \end{array}$$

5)
$$\begin{array}{r} 60 \\ + 61 \\ \hline \end{array}$$

6)
$$\begin{array}{r} 19 \\ + 34 \\ \hline \end{array}$$

7)
$$\begin{array}{r} 43 \\ + 50 \\ \hline \end{array}$$

8)
$$\begin{array}{r} 16 \\ + 40 \\ \hline \end{array}$$

9)
$$\begin{array}{r} 97 \\ + 56 \\ \hline \end{array}$$

10)
$$\begin{array}{r} 14 \\ + 45 \\ \hline \end{array}$$

11)
$$\begin{array}{r} 28 \\ + 34 \\ \hline \end{array}$$

12)
$$\begin{array}{r} 88 \\ + 82 \\ \hline \end{array}$$

13)
$$\begin{array}{r} 30 \\ + 35 \\ \hline \end{array}$$

14)
$$\begin{array}{r} 72 \\ + 31 \\ \hline \end{array}$$

15)
$$\begin{array}{r} 10 \\ + 62 \\ \hline \end{array}$$

16)
$$\begin{array}{r} 38 \\ + 45 \\ \hline \end{array}$$

17)
$$\begin{array}{r} 94 \\ + 56 \\ \hline \end{array}$$

18)
$$\begin{array}{r} 38 \\ + 47 \\ \hline \end{array}$$

19)
$$\begin{array}{r} 22 \\ + 91 \\ \hline \end{array}$$

20)
$$\begin{array}{r} 59 \\ + 14 \\ \hline \end{array}$$

21)
$$\begin{array}{r} 91 \\ + 59 \\ \hline \end{array}$$

22)
$$\begin{array}{r} 84 \\ + 74 \\ \hline \end{array}$$

23)
$$\begin{array}{r} 60 \\ + 92 \\ \hline \end{array}$$

24)
$$\begin{array}{r} 70 \\ + 58 \\ \hline \end{array}$$

25)
$$\begin{array}{r} 55 \\ + 86 \\ \hline \end{array}$$

26)
$$\begin{array}{r} 68 \\ + 54 \\ \hline \end{array}$$

27)
$$\begin{array}{r} 44 \\ + 15 \\ \hline \end{array}$$

28)
$$\begin{array}{r} 65 \\ + 87 \\ \hline \end{array}$$

29)
$$\begin{array}{r} 64 \\ + 34 \\ \hline \end{array}$$

30)
$$\begin{array}{r} 85 \\ + 13 \\ \hline \end{array}$$

1) 27
  + 93

2) 84
  + 41

3) 29
  + 46

4) 42
  + 66

5) 81
  + 44

6) 83
  + 35

7) 76
  + 86

8) 46
  + 25

9) 94
  + 57

10) 92
  + 18

11) 61
  + 10

12) 45
  + 32

13) 62
  + 54

14) 96
  + 17

15) 40
  + 79

16) 77
  + 13

17) 62
  + 39

18) 77
  + 72

19) 19
  + 36

20) 93
  + 22

21) 56
  + 12

22) 82
  + 73

23) 82
  + 51

24) 97
  + 93

25) 87
  + 51

26) 19
  + 96

27) 90
  + 96

28) 29
  + 42

29) 23
  + 37

30) 36
  + 87

1) 41
  + 35

2) 40
  + 43

3) 15
  + 53

4) 98
  + 74

5) 32
  + 52

6) 52
  + 61

7) 56
  + 56

8) 71
  + 87

9) 59
  + 23

10) 98
  + 99

11) 92
  + 84

12) 76
  + 45

13) 97
  + 56

14) 53
  + 82

15) 46
  + 10

16) 88
  + 68

17) 54
  + 55

18) 96
  + 58

19) 58
  + 27

20) 54
  + 79

21) 14
  + 76

22) 14
  + 47

23) 37
  + 69

24) 56
  + 43

25) 89
  + 53

26) 20
  + 69

27) 68
  + 63

28) 95
  + 12

29) 94
  + 77

30) 37
  + 93

1)   68
 + 42

2)   45
 + 41

3)   49
 + 11

4)   70
 + 71

5)   73
 + 20

6)   63
 + 55

7)   35
 + 42

8)   24
 + 21

9)   38
 + 37

10)   75
 + 37

11)   91
 + 18

12)   25
 + 42

13)   43
 + 72

14)   92
 + 49

15)   22
 + 56

16)   11
 + 42

17)   54
 + 86

18)   72
 + 62

19)   63
 + 76

20)   14
 + 32

21)   12
 + 67

22)   54
 + 63

23)   59
 + 77

24)   87
 + 59

25)   50
 + 49

26)   47
 + 86

27)   16
 + 25

28)   15
 + 78

29)   85
 + 31

30)   42
 + 29

Subtraction

Subtract 1-digit from
2-digit numbers
in columns
and write the
correct answer!

1) 14 − 1

2) 78 − 7

3) 70 − 1

4) 36 − 5

5) 28 − 6

6) 16 − 9

7) 36 − 6

8) 63 − 4

9) 77 − 7

10) 19 − 5

11) 49 − 2

12) 45 − 5

13) 46 − 7

14) 39 − 5

15) 79 − 3

16) 50 − 1

17) 17 − 1

18) 65 − 1

19) 80 − 3

20) 84 − 3

21) 48 − 8

22) 96 − 3

23) 17 − 3

24) 33 − 6

25) 98 − 5

26) 79 − 9

27) 28 − 2

28) 21 − 9

29) 21 − 6

30) 67 − 9

1)   35
   − 2
   ____

2)   59
   − 1
   ____

3)   96
   − 1
   ____

4)   40
   − 9
   ____

5)   45
   − 9
   ____

6)   13
   − 4
   ____

7)   16
   − 6
   ____

8)   88
   − 8
   ____

9)   57
   − 2
   ____

10) 61
   − 1
   ____

11) 51
   − 9
   ____

12) 52
   − 8
   ____

13) 99
   − 2
   ____

14) 32
   − 5
   ____

15) 58
   − 2
   ____

16) 53
   − 7
   ____

17) 76
   − 7
   ____

18) 51
   − 3
   ____

19) 29
   − 9
   ____

20) 13
   − 6
   ____

21) 46
   − 3
   ____

22) 62
   − 5
   ____

23) 85
   − 9
   ____

24) 46
   − 8
   ____

25) 68
   − 4
   ____

26) 71
   − 3
   ____

27) 28
   − 3
   ____

28) 12
   − 2
   ____

29) 69
   − 1
   ____

30) 27
   − 5
   ____

1)
```
  30
-  5
----
```

2)
```
  43
-  1
----
```

3)
```
  97
-  5
----
```

4)
```
  28
-  9
----
```

5)
```
  45
-  4
----
```

6)
```
  55
-  2
----
```

7)
```
  76
-  1
----
```

8)
```
  84
-  6
----
```

9)
```
  34
-  8
----
```

10)
```
  19
-  2
----
```

11)
```
  82
-  3
----
```

12)
```
  74
-  4
----
```

13)
```
  80
-  8
----
```

14)
```
  29
-  2
----
```

15)
```
  57
-  2
----
```

16)
```
  53
-  3
----
```

17)
```
  69
-  8
----
```

18)
```
  87
-  3
----
```

19)
```
  98
-  5
----
```

20)
```
  57
-  7
----
```

21)
```
  77
-  9
----
```

22)
```
  61
-  5
----
```

23)
```
  59
-  7
----
```

24)
```
  21
-  4
----
```

25)
```
  17
-  4
----
```

26)
```
  99
-  3
----
```

27)
```
  29
-  3
----
```

28)
```
  51
-  6
----
```

29)
```
  75
-  9
----
```

30)
```
  98
-  6
----
```

1) 50 − 2

2) 66 − 9

3) 99 − 1

4) 27 − 2

5) 77 − 4

6) 88 − 2

7) 63 − 5

8) 74 − 6

9) 46 − 2

10) 89 − 8

11) 12 − 8

12) 90 − 6

13) 49 − 6

14) 85 − 9

15) 79 − 5

16) 52 − 2

17) 81 − 7

18) 18 − 3

19) 16 − 6

20) 86 − 1

21) 20 − 5

22) 69 − 5

23) 34 − 6

24) 85 − 1

25) 81 − 1

26) 91 − 1

27) 64 − 3

28) 94 − 3

29) 69 − 4

30) 71 − 8

1)   69
   − 3
   ____

2)   98
   − 1
   ____

3)   95
   − 4
   ____

4)   46
   − 5
   ____

5)   10
   − 3
   ____

6)   69
   − 8
   ____

7)   82
   − 6
   ____

8)   98
   − 1
   ____

9)   71
   − 4
   ____

10)   25
   − 6
   ____

11)   71
   − 4
   ____

12)   61
   − 7
   ____

13)   37
   − 6
   ____

14)   11
   − 3
   ____

15)   95
   − 9
   ____

16)   66
   − 3
   ____

17)   42
   − 7
   ____

18)   29
   − 4
   ____

19)   20
   − 5
   ____

20)   54
   − 4
   ____

21)   33
   − 3
   ____

22)   71
   − 5
   ____

23)   24
   − 8
   ____

24)   80
   − 6
   ____

25)   40
   − 1
   ____

26)   28
   − 4
   ____

27)   52
   − 3
   ____

28)   77
   − 5
   ____

29)   31
   − 5
   ____

30)   89
   − 2
   ____

1) 17 − 7

2) 18 − 9

3) 28 − 3

4) 36 − 8

5) 56 − 7

6) 14 − 3

7) 76 − 5

8) 77 − 5

9) 38 − 3

10) 59 − 6

11) 73 − 6

12) 96 − 4

13) 57 − 4

14) 86 − 9

15) 40 − 8

16) 60 − 7

17) 26 − 4

18) 11 − 5

19) 28 − 2

20) 58 − 6

21) 15 − 2

22) 42 − 5

23) 88 − 9

24) 36 − 3

25) 89 − 8

26) 60 − 5

27) 54 − 3

28) 69 − 4

29) 81 − 4

30) 14 − 6

1) 38 − 4

2) 71 − 5

3) 41 − 4

4) 99 − 5

5) 70 − 1

6) 75 − 3

7) 99 − 9

8) 54 − 6

9) 54 − 9

10) 41 − 9

11) 14 − 5

12) 25 − 5

13) 21 − 8

14) 77 − 9

15) 70 − 4

16) 45 − 6

17) 44 − 7

18) 91 − 8

19) 66 − 8

20) 14 − 2

21) 11 − 3

22) 95 − 5

23) 69 − 5

24) 75 − 5

25) 18 − 4

26) 66 − 5

27) 29 − 7

28) 90 − 1

29) 47 − 6

30) 32 − 7

1)
$$35 - 1$$

2)
$$12 - 8$$

3)
$$15 - 9$$

4)
$$62 - 4$$

5)
$$46 - 4$$

6)
$$57 - 5$$

7)
$$35 - 3$$

8)
$$12 - 1$$

9)
$$30 - 6$$

10)
$$33 - 1$$

11)
$$73 - 6$$

12)
$$83 - 3$$

13)
$$60 - 2$$

14)
$$31 - 5$$

15)
$$47 - 2$$

16)
$$40 - 8$$

17)
$$18 - 1$$

18)
$$89 - 7$$

19)
$$28 - 6$$

20)
$$95 - 1$$

21)
$$96 - 3$$

22)
$$29 - 4$$

23)
$$50 - 5$$

24)
$$42 - 5$$

25)
$$16 - 2$$

26)
$$97 - 6$$

27)
$$37 - 6$$

28)
$$69 - 4$$

29)
$$41 - 7$$

30)
$$16 - 1$$

Subtraction

Subtract
2-digit numbers
in columns
and write the
correct answer!

1) 89 − 36

2) 59 − 37

3) 89 − 89

4) 60 − 41

5) 38 − 38

6) 62 − 54

7) 80 − 49

8) 96 − 86

9) 46 − 35

10) 36 − 13

11) 77 − 19

12) 83 − 18

13) 87 − 66

14) 56 − 29

15) 64 − 29

16) 66 − 15

17) 69 − 53

18) 55 − 55

19) 67 − 31

20) 64 − 35

21) 75 − 47

22) 99 − 43

23) 75 − 44

24) 72 − 56

25) 50 − 18

26) 56 − 42

27) 52 − 51

28) 72 − 41

29) 70 − 46

30) 42 − 13

1)　　67
　　− 44
　　‾‾‾‾

2)　　59
　　− 14
　　‾‾‾‾

3)　　95
　　− 16
　　‾‾‾‾

4)　　61
　　− 23
　　‾‾‾‾

5)　　58
　　− 14
　　‾‾‾‾

6)　　54
　　− 44
　　‾‾‾‾

7)　　46
　　− 32
　　‾‾‾‾

8)　　69
　　− 39
　　‾‾‾‾

9)　　71
　　− 43
　　‾‾‾‾

10)　　65
　　− 33
　　‾‾‾‾

11)　　80
　　− 24
　　‾‾‾‾

12)　　70
　　− 20
　　‾‾‾‾

13)　　78
　　− 63
　　‾‾‾‾

14)　　92
　　− 63
　　‾‾‾‾

15)　　74
　　− 19
　　‾‾‾‾

16)　　62
　　− 59
　　‾‾‾‾

17)　　99
　　− 24
　　‾‾‾‾

18)　　38
　　− 12
　　‾‾‾‾

19)　　96
　　− 31
　　‾‾‾‾

20)　　84
　　− 55
　　‾‾‾‾

21)　　65
　　− 55
　　‾‾‾‾

22)　　42
　　− 12
　　‾‾‾‾

23)　　81
　　− 44
　　‾‾‾‾

24)　　79
　　− 38
　　‾‾‾‾

25)　　66
　　− 43
　　‾‾‾‾

26)　　36
　　− 34
　　‾‾‾‾

27)　　93
　　− 51
　　‾‾‾‾

28)　　71
　　− 17
　　‾‾‾‾

29)　　97
　　− 71
　　‾‾‾‾

30)　　71
　　− 23
　　‾‾‾‾

1) $\begin{array}{r} 82 \\ -\ 43 \\ \hline \end{array}$
2) $\begin{array}{r} 55 \\ -\ 30 \\ \hline \end{array}$
3) $\begin{array}{r} 68 \\ -\ 61 \\ \hline \end{array}$
4) $\begin{array}{r} 72 \\ -\ 54 \\ \hline \end{array}$
5) $\begin{array}{r} 76 \\ -\ 61 \\ \hline \end{array}$

6) $\begin{array}{r} 85 \\ -\ 53 \\ \hline \end{array}$
7) $\begin{array}{r} 59 \\ -\ 31 \\ \hline \end{array}$
8) $\begin{array}{r} 99 \\ -\ 70 \\ \hline \end{array}$
9) $\begin{array}{r} 78 \\ -\ 74 \\ \hline \end{array}$
10) $\begin{array}{r} 49 \\ -\ 10 \\ \hline \end{array}$

11) $\begin{array}{r} 85 \\ -\ 23 \\ \hline \end{array}$
12) $\begin{array}{r} 25 \\ -\ 20 \\ \hline \end{array}$
13) $\begin{array}{r} 94 \\ -\ 13 \\ \hline \end{array}$
14) $\begin{array}{r} 75 \\ -\ 10 \\ \hline \end{array}$
15) $\begin{array}{r} 76 \\ -\ 56 \\ \hline \end{array}$

16) $\begin{array}{r} 60 \\ -\ 48 \\ \hline \end{array}$
17) $\begin{array}{r} 98 \\ -\ 95 \\ \hline \end{array}$
18) $\begin{array}{r} 54 \\ -\ 51 \\ \hline \end{array}$
19) $\begin{array}{r} 40 \\ -\ 11 \\ \hline \end{array}$
20) $\begin{array}{r} 84 \\ -\ 11 \\ \hline \end{array}$

21) $\begin{array}{r} 55 \\ -\ 19 \\ \hline \end{array}$
22) $\begin{array}{r} 66 \\ -\ 39 \\ \hline \end{array}$
23) $\begin{array}{r} 72 \\ -\ 26 \\ \hline \end{array}$
24) $\begin{array}{r} 41 \\ -\ 33 \\ \hline \end{array}$
25) $\begin{array}{r} 42 \\ -\ 26 \\ \hline \end{array}$

26) $\begin{array}{r} 90 \\ -\ 28 \\ \hline \end{array}$
27) $\begin{array}{r} 74 \\ -\ 62 \\ \hline \end{array}$
28) $\begin{array}{r} 84 \\ -\ 33 \\ \hline \end{array}$
29) $\begin{array}{r} 82 \\ -\ 31 \\ \hline \end{array}$
30) $\begin{array}{r} 71 \\ -\ 42 \\ \hline \end{array}$

1) 42 − 31

2) 54 − 30

3) 45 − 11

4) 35 − 10

5) 43 − 33

6) 83 − 37

7) 94 − 88

8) 57 − 10

9) 50 − 49

10) 96 − 47

11) 94 − 57

12) 91 − 18

13) 76 − 64

14) 73 − 50

15) 87 − 30

16) 69 − 22

17) 98 − 84

18) 63 − 23

19) 88 − 33

20) 94 − 16

21) 97 − 82

22) 54 − 30

23) 84 − 82

24) 96 − 32

25) 41 − 12

26) 42 − 32

27) 62 − 37

28) 90 − 18

29) 92 − 49

30) 54 − 13

1) 28
  − 18

2) 53
  − 33

3) 93
  − 42

4) 30
  − 12

5) 61
  − 16

6) 24
  − 24

7) 79
  − 65

8) 93
  − 79

9) 33
  − 18

10) 94
  − 45

11) 86
  − 24

12) 90
  − 27

13) 49
  − 13

14) 69
  − 68

15) 68
  − 10

16) 92
  − 29

17) 69
  − 33

18) 94
  − 93

19) 93
  − 93

20) 40
  − 19

21) 78
  − 49

22) 65
  − 39

23) 48
  − 28

24) 52
  − 18

25) 98
  − 51

26) 95
  − 68

27) 80
  − 67

28) 71
  − 47

29) 97
  − 77

30) 53
  − 37

1)
$$42 - 33$$

2)
$$71 - 57$$

3)
$$41 - 27$$

4)
$$67 - 16$$

5)
$$91 - 17$$

6)
$$87 - 20$$

7)
$$92 - 88$$

8)
$$86 - 84$$

9)
$$79 - 45$$

10)
$$54 - 23$$

11)
$$71 - 16$$

12)
$$90 - 84$$

13)
$$50 - 16$$

14)
$$74 - 28$$

15)
$$80 - 38$$

16)
$$48 - 30$$

17)
$$75 - 53$$

18)
$$82 - 52$$

19)
$$76 - 24$$

20)
$$17 - 10$$

21)
$$99 - 31$$

22)
$$65 - 25$$

23)
$$51 - 10$$

24)
$$45 - 42$$

25)
$$76 - 47$$

26)
$$63 - 37$$

27)
$$48 - 43$$

28)
$$83 - 30$$

29)
$$24 - 12$$

30)
$$95 - 69$$

1) 71
  − 18

2) 34
  − 26

3) 82
  − 81

4) 75
  − 55

5) 49
  − 36

6) 98
  − 69

7) 46
  − 29

8) 50
  − 12

9) 88
  − 40

10) 78
  − 28

11) 36
  − 28

12) 94
  − 29

13) 64
  − 14

14) 30
  − 23

15) 65
  − 29

16) 94
  − 91

17) 87
  − 30

18) 53
  − 38

19) 61
  − 31

20) 96
  − 89

21) 99
  − 63

22) 85
  − 26

23) 98
  − 52

24) 96
  − 53

25) 42
  − 16

26) 37
  − 30

27) 76
  − 68

28) 78
  − 54

29) 83
  − 51

30) 98
  − 65

1)	$\begin{array}{r}77\\-28\\\hline\end{array}$	2)	$\begin{array}{r}82\\-78\\\hline\end{array}$	3)	$\begin{array}{r}82\\-61\\\hline\end{array}$	4)	$\begin{array}{r}63\\-48\\\hline\end{array}$	5)	$\begin{array}{r}67\\-66\\\hline\end{array}$
6)	$\begin{array}{r}21\\-20\\\hline\end{array}$	7)	$\begin{array}{r}45\\-19\\\hline\end{array}$	8)	$\begin{array}{r}87\\-18\\\hline\end{array}$	9)	$\begin{array}{r}90\\-43\\\hline\end{array}$	10)	$\begin{array}{r}60\\-47\\\hline\end{array}$
11)	$\begin{array}{r}88\\-58\\\hline\end{array}$	12)	$\begin{array}{r}97\\-19\\\hline\end{array}$	13)	$\begin{array}{r}41\\-16\\\hline\end{array}$	14)	$\begin{array}{r}92\\-42\\\hline\end{array}$	15)	$\begin{array}{r}91\\-89\\\hline\end{array}$
16)	$\begin{array}{r}40\\-37\\\hline\end{array}$	17)	$\begin{array}{r}73\\-59\\\hline\end{array}$	18)	$\begin{array}{r}25\\-25\\\hline\end{array}$	19)	$\begin{array}{r}74\\-25\\\hline\end{array}$	20)	$\begin{array}{r}93\\-58\\\hline\end{array}$
21)	$\begin{array}{r}76\\-22\\\hline\end{array}$	22)	$\begin{array}{r}95\\-66\\\hline\end{array}$	23)	$\begin{array}{r}56\\-45\\\hline\end{array}$	24)	$\begin{array}{r}39\\-22\\\hline\end{array}$	25)	$\begin{array}{r}85\\-18\\\hline\end{array}$
26)	$\begin{array}{r}66\\-61\\\hline\end{array}$	27)	$\begin{array}{r}66\\-47\\\hline\end{array}$	28)	$\begin{array}{r}33\\-15\\\hline\end{array}$	29)	$\begin{array}{r}69\\-68\\\hline\end{array}$	30)	$\begin{array}{r}80\\-56\\\hline\end{array}$

Times Tables 1-5

Multiply numbers from 0 to 10 with numbers from 1 to 5 in columns!

1)
```
      3
×     4
─────────
```

2)
```
      9
×     2
─────────
```

3)
```
     10
×     5
─────────
```

4)
```
      9
×     5
─────────
```

5)
```
      7
×     2
─────────
```

6)
```
      7
×     3
─────────
```

7)
```
      6
×     2
─────────
```

8)
```
      6
×     3
─────────
```

9)
```
      2
×     3
─────────
```

10)
```
      7
×     4
─────────
```

11)
```
      7
×     4
─────────
```

12)
```
      2
×     3
─────────
```

13)
```
      3
×     1
─────────
```

14)
```
      8
×     1
─────────
```

15)
```
      1
×     3
─────────
```

16)
```
     10
×     2
─────────
```

17)
```
      9
×     4
─────────
```

18)
```
     10
×     2
─────────
```

19)
```
      5
×     1
─────────
```

20)
```
      1
×     1
─────────
```

21)
```
      5
×     5
─────────
```

22)
```
      8
×     3
─────────
```

23)
```
      4
×     3
─────────
```

24)
```
      2
×     5
─────────
```

25)
```
     10
×     5
─────────
```

26)
```
      8
×     3
─────────
```

27)
```
      9
×     1
─────────
```

28)
```
      3
×     3
─────────
```

29)
```
      2
×     3
─────────
```

30)
```
     10
×     3
─────────
```

1)
$$\begin{array}{r} 4 \\ \times\ 1 \\ \hline \end{array}$$

2)
$$\begin{array}{r} 4 \\ \times\ 4 \\ \hline \end{array}$$

3)
$$\begin{array}{r} 1 \\ \times\ 3 \\ \hline \end{array}$$

4)
$$\begin{array}{r} 9 \\ \times\ 4 \\ \hline \end{array}$$

5)
$$\begin{array}{r} 5 \\ \times\ 5 \\ \hline \end{array}$$

6)
$$\begin{array}{r} 4 \\ \times\ 5 \\ \hline \end{array}$$

7)
$$\begin{array}{r} 2 \\ \times\ 4 \\ \hline \end{array}$$

8)
$$\begin{array}{r} 2 \\ \times\ 2 \\ \hline \end{array}$$

9)
$$\begin{array}{r} 2 \\ \times\ 2 \\ \hline \end{array}$$

10)
$$\begin{array}{r} 3 \\ \times\ 5 \\ \hline \end{array}$$

11)
$$\begin{array}{r} 1 \\ \times\ 4 \\ \hline \end{array}$$

12)
$$\begin{array}{r} 5 \\ \times\ 2 \\ \hline \end{array}$$

13)
$$\begin{array}{r} 3 \\ \times\ 4 \\ \hline \end{array}$$

14)
$$\begin{array}{r} 6 \\ \times\ 3 \\ \hline \end{array}$$

15)
$$\begin{array}{r} 6 \\ \times\ 3 \\ \hline \end{array}$$

16)
$$\begin{array}{r} 2 \\ \times\ 1 \\ \hline \end{array}$$

17)
$$\begin{array}{r} 8 \\ \times\ 5 \\ \hline \end{array}$$

18)
$$\begin{array}{r} 3 \\ \times\ 1 \\ \hline \end{array}$$

19)
$$\begin{array}{r} 4 \\ \times\ 3 \\ \hline \end{array}$$

20)
$$\begin{array}{r} 7 \\ \times\ 5 \\ \hline \end{array}$$

21)
$$\begin{array}{r} 5 \\ \times\ 3 \\ \hline \end{array}$$

22)
$$\begin{array}{r} 4 \\ \times\ 1 \\ \hline \end{array}$$

23)
$$\begin{array}{r} 4 \\ \times\ 4 \\ \hline \end{array}$$

24)
$$\begin{array}{r} 1 \\ \times\ 2 \\ \hline \end{array}$$

25)
$$\begin{array}{r} 2 \\ \times\ 1 \\ \hline \end{array}$$

26)
$$\begin{array}{r} 5 \\ \times\ 1 \\ \hline \end{array}$$

27)
$$\begin{array}{r} 9 \\ \times\ 5 \\ \hline \end{array}$$

28)
$$\begin{array}{r} 2 \\ \times\ 1 \\ \hline \end{array}$$

29)
$$\begin{array}{r} 2 \\ \times\ 1 \\ \hline \end{array}$$

30)
$$\begin{array}{r} 10 \\ \times\ 3 \\ \hline \end{array}$$

1)
$$\begin{array}{r} 3 \\ \times\ 5 \\ \hline \end{array}$$

2)
$$\begin{array}{r} 10 \\ \times\ 2 \\ \hline \end{array}$$

3)
$$\begin{array}{r} 10 \\ \times\ 4 \\ \hline \end{array}$$

4)
$$\begin{array}{r} 3 \\ \times\ 5 \\ \hline \end{array}$$

5)
$$\begin{array}{r} 10 \\ \times\ 3 \\ \hline \end{array}$$

6)
$$\begin{array}{r} 7 \\ \times\ 5 \\ \hline \end{array}$$

7)
$$\begin{array}{r} 5 \\ \times\ 2 \\ \hline \end{array}$$

8)
$$\begin{array}{r} 8 \\ \times\ 5 \\ \hline \end{array}$$

9)
$$\begin{array}{r} 6 \\ \times\ 1 \\ \hline \end{array}$$

10)
$$\begin{array}{r} 8 \\ \times\ 5 \\ \hline \end{array}$$

11)
$$\begin{array}{r} 8 \\ \times\ 2 \\ \hline \end{array}$$

12)
$$\begin{array}{r} 2 \\ \times\ 3 \\ \hline \end{array}$$

13)
$$\begin{array}{r} 1 \\ \times\ 3 \\ \hline \end{array}$$

14)
$$\begin{array}{r} 10 \\ \times\ 3 \\ \hline \end{array}$$

15)
$$\begin{array}{r} 5 \\ \times\ 1 \\ \hline \end{array}$$

16)
$$\begin{array}{r} 4 \\ \times\ 5 \\ \hline \end{array}$$

17)
$$\begin{array}{r} 3 \\ \times\ 2 \\ \hline \end{array}$$

18)
$$\begin{array}{r} 5 \\ \times\ 1 \\ \hline \end{array}$$

19)
$$\begin{array}{r} 2 \\ \times\ 1 \\ \hline \end{array}$$

20)
$$\begin{array}{r} 8 \\ \times\ 5 \\ \hline \end{array}$$

21)
$$\begin{array}{r} 10 \\ \times\ 5 \\ \hline \end{array}$$

22)
$$\begin{array}{r} 7 \\ \times\ 4 \\ \hline \end{array}$$

23)
$$\begin{array}{r} 10 \\ \times\ 2 \\ \hline \end{array}$$

24)
$$\begin{array}{r} 1 \\ \times\ 1 \\ \hline \end{array}$$

25)
$$\begin{array}{r} 7 \\ \times\ 5 \\ \hline \end{array}$$

26)
$$\begin{array}{r} 2 \\ \times\ 2 \\ \hline \end{array}$$

27)
$$\begin{array}{r} 9 \\ \times\ 4 \\ \hline \end{array}$$

28)
$$\begin{array}{r} 9 \\ \times\ 5 \\ \hline \end{array}$$

29)
$$\begin{array}{r} 9 \\ \times\ 5 \\ \hline \end{array}$$

30)
$$\begin{array}{r} 8 \\ \times\ 5 \\ \hline \end{array}$$

1)
$$\begin{array}{r} 6 \\ \times\ 3 \\ \hline \end{array}$$

2)
$$\begin{array}{r} 4 \\ \times\ 2 \\ \hline \end{array}$$

3)
$$\begin{array}{r} 7 \\ \times\ 4 \\ \hline \end{array}$$

4)
$$\begin{array}{r} 9 \\ \times\ 3 \\ \hline \end{array}$$

5)
$$\begin{array}{r} 9 \\ \times\ 3 \\ \hline \end{array}$$

6)
$$\begin{array}{r} 8 \\ \times\ 3 \\ \hline \end{array}$$

7)
$$\begin{array}{r} 4 \\ \times\ 2 \\ \hline \end{array}$$

8)
$$\begin{array}{r} 1 \\ \times\ 1 \\ \hline \end{array}$$

9)
$$\begin{array}{r} 6 \\ \times\ 4 \\ \hline \end{array}$$

10)
$$\begin{array}{r} 5 \\ \times\ 2 \\ \hline \end{array}$$

11)
$$\begin{array}{r} 5 \\ \times\ 1 \\ \hline \end{array}$$

12)
$$\begin{array}{r} 5 \\ \times\ 3 \\ \hline \end{array}$$

13)
$$\begin{array}{r} 6 \\ \times\ 4 \\ \hline \end{array}$$

14)
$$\begin{array}{r} 6 \\ \times\ 2 \\ \hline \end{array}$$

15)
$$\begin{array}{r} 7 \\ \times\ 2 \\ \hline \end{array}$$

16)
$$\begin{array}{r} 9 \\ \times\ 3 \\ \hline \end{array}$$

17)
$$\begin{array}{r} 10 \\ \times\ 4 \\ \hline \end{array}$$

18)
$$\begin{array}{r} 5 \\ \times\ 5 \\ \hline \end{array}$$

19)
$$\begin{array}{r} 2 \\ \times\ 4 \\ \hline \end{array}$$

20)
$$\begin{array}{r} 4 \\ \times\ 3 \\ \hline \end{array}$$

21)
$$\begin{array}{r} 5 \\ \times\ 4 \\ \hline \end{array}$$

22)
$$\begin{array}{r} 7 \\ \times\ 1 \\ \hline \end{array}$$

23)
$$\begin{array}{r} 6 \\ \times\ 1 \\ \hline \end{array}$$

24)
$$\begin{array}{r} 5 \\ \times\ 3 \\ \hline \end{array}$$

25)
$$\begin{array}{r} 9 \\ \times\ 4 \\ \hline \end{array}$$

26)
$$\begin{array}{r} 10 \\ \times\ 2 \\ \hline \end{array}$$

27)
$$\begin{array}{r} 4 \\ \times\ 2 \\ \hline \end{array}$$

28)
$$\begin{array}{r} 3 \\ \times\ 4 \\ \hline \end{array}$$

29)
$$\begin{array}{r} 8 \\ \times\ 2 \\ \hline \end{array}$$

30)
$$\begin{array}{r} 7 \\ \times\ 4 \\ \hline \end{array}$$

1)
$$\begin{array}{r} 7 \\ \times\ 4 \\ \hline \end{array}$$

2)
$$\begin{array}{r} 2 \\ \times\ 5 \\ \hline \end{array}$$

3)
$$\begin{array}{r} 5 \\ \times\ 3 \\ \hline \end{array}$$

4)
$$\begin{array}{r} 2 \\ \times\ 2 \\ \hline \end{array}$$

5)
$$\begin{array}{r} 5 \\ \times\ 1 \\ \hline \end{array}$$

6)
$$\begin{array}{r} 1 \\ \times\ 3 \\ \hline \end{array}$$

7)
$$\begin{array}{r} 7 \\ \times\ 2 \\ \hline \end{array}$$

8)
$$\begin{array}{r} 4 \\ \times\ 3 \\ \hline \end{array}$$

9)
$$\begin{array}{r} 8 \\ \times\ 1 \\ \hline \end{array}$$

10)
$$\begin{array}{r} 8 \\ \times\ 1 \\ \hline \end{array}$$

11)
$$\begin{array}{r} 8 \\ \times\ 5 \\ \hline \end{array}$$

12)
$$\begin{array}{r} 1 \\ \times\ 4 \\ \hline \end{array}$$

13)
$$\begin{array}{r} 2 \\ \times\ 1 \\ \hline \end{array}$$

14)
$$\begin{array}{r} 1 \\ \times\ 2 \\ \hline \end{array}$$

15)
$$\begin{array}{r} 3 \\ \times\ 4 \\ \hline \end{array}$$

16)
$$\begin{array}{r} 6 \\ \times\ 2 \\ \hline \end{array}$$

17)
$$\begin{array}{r} 1 \\ \times\ 3 \\ \hline \end{array}$$

18)
$$\begin{array}{r} 7 \\ \times\ 2 \\ \hline \end{array}$$

19)
$$\begin{array}{r} 10 \\ \times\ 1 \\ \hline \end{array}$$

20)
$$\begin{array}{r} 3 \\ \times\ 5 \\ \hline \end{array}$$

21)
$$\begin{array}{r} 3 \\ \times\ 1 \\ \hline \end{array}$$

22)
$$\begin{array}{r} 10 \\ \times\ 5 \\ \hline \end{array}$$

23)
$$\begin{array}{r} 2 \\ \times\ 1 \\ \hline \end{array}$$

24)
$$\begin{array}{r} 3 \\ \times\ 1 \\ \hline \end{array}$$

25)
$$\begin{array}{r} 6 \\ \times\ 2 \\ \hline \end{array}$$

26)
$$\begin{array}{r} 4 \\ \times\ 5 \\ \hline \end{array}$$

27)
$$\begin{array}{r} 9 \\ \times\ 3 \\ \hline \end{array}$$

28)
$$\begin{array}{r} 3 \\ \times\ 5 \\ \hline \end{array}$$

29)
$$\begin{array}{r} 10 \\ \times\ 1 \\ \hline \end{array}$$

30)
$$\begin{array}{r} 8 \\ \times\ 4 \\ \hline \end{array}$$

1) 7 × 5

2) 9 × 5

3) 8 × 3

4) 9 × 5

5) 1 × 4

6) 9 × 5

7) 3 × 5

8) 9 × 2

9) 6 × 4

10) 2 × 2

11) 3 × 3

12) 10 × 1

13) 4 × 5

14) 3 × 2

15) 6 × 1

16) 5 × 1

17) 7 × 2

18) 2 × 2

19) 1 × 1

20) 7 × 1

21) 3 × 5

22) 3 × 4

23) 6 × 5

24) 10 × 5

25) 6 × 1

26) 2 × 2

27) 6 × 3

28) 7 × 3

29) 10 × 3

30) 2 × 1

1)
$$\begin{array}{r} 8 \\ \times\ 1 \\ \hline \end{array}$$

2)
$$\begin{array}{r} 2 \\ \times\ 4 \\ \hline \end{array}$$

3)
$$\begin{array}{r} 6 \\ \times\ 1 \\ \hline \end{array}$$

4)
$$\begin{array}{r} 9 \\ \times\ 5 \\ \hline \end{array}$$

5)
$$\begin{array}{r} 7 \\ \times\ 5 \\ \hline \end{array}$$

6)
$$\begin{array}{r} 4 \\ \times\ 5 \\ \hline \end{array}$$

7)
$$\begin{array}{r} 4 \\ \times\ 2 \\ \hline \end{array}$$

8)
$$\begin{array}{r} 10 \\ \times\ 2 \\ \hline \end{array}$$

9)
$$\begin{array}{r} 3 \\ \times\ 1 \\ \hline \end{array}$$

10)
$$\begin{array}{r} 7 \\ \times\ 2 \\ \hline \end{array}$$

11)
$$\begin{array}{r} 8 \\ \times\ 5 \\ \hline \end{array}$$

12)
$$\begin{array}{r} 6 \\ \times\ 5 \\ \hline \end{array}$$

13)
$$\begin{array}{r} 6 \\ \times\ 4 \\ \hline \end{array}$$

14)
$$\begin{array}{r} 3 \\ \times\ 5 \\ \hline \end{array}$$

15)
$$\begin{array}{r} 10 \\ \times\ 2 \\ \hline \end{array}$$

16)
$$\begin{array}{r} 7 \\ \times\ 3 \\ \hline \end{array}$$

17)
$$\begin{array}{r} 8 \\ \times\ 2 \\ \hline \end{array}$$

18)
$$\begin{array}{r} 1 \\ \times\ 2 \\ \hline \end{array}$$

19)
$$\begin{array}{r} 10 \\ \times\ 3 \\ \hline \end{array}$$

20)
$$\begin{array}{r} 7 \\ \times\ 4 \\ \hline \end{array}$$

21)
$$\begin{array}{r} 7 \\ \times\ 2 \\ \hline \end{array}$$

22)
$$\begin{array}{r} 5 \\ \times\ 3 \\ \hline \end{array}$$

23)
$$\begin{array}{r} 2 \\ \times\ 5 \\ \hline \end{array}$$

24)
$$\begin{array}{r} 7 \\ \times\ 4 \\ \hline \end{array}$$

25)
$$\begin{array}{r} 9 \\ \times\ 4 \\ \hline \end{array}$$

26)
$$\begin{array}{r} 4 \\ \times\ 4 \\ \hline \end{array}$$

27)
$$\begin{array}{r} 3 \\ \times\ 3 \\ \hline \end{array}$$

28)
$$\begin{array}{r} 1 \\ \times\ 4 \\ \hline \end{array}$$

29)
$$\begin{array}{r} 6 \\ \times\ 1 \\ \hline \end{array}$$

30)
$$\begin{array}{r} 2 \\ \times\ 2 \\ \hline \end{array}$$

1)
$$\begin{array}{r} 1 \\ \times\ \ 3 \\ \hline \end{array}$$

2)
$$\begin{array}{r} 5 \\ \times\ \ 2 \\ \hline \end{array}$$

3)
$$\begin{array}{r} 5 \\ \times\ \ 3 \\ \hline \end{array}$$

4)
$$\begin{array}{r} 7 \\ \times\ \ 4 \\ \hline \end{array}$$

5)
$$\begin{array}{r} 6 \\ \times\ \ 3 \\ \hline \end{array}$$

6)
$$\begin{array}{r} 10 \\ \times\ \ 2 \\ \hline \end{array}$$

7)
$$\begin{array}{r} 10 \\ \times\ \ 2 \\ \hline \end{array}$$

8)
$$\begin{array}{r} 8 \\ \times\ \ 1 \\ \hline \end{array}$$

9)
$$\begin{array}{r} 9 \\ \times\ \ 2 \\ \hline \end{array}$$

10)
$$\begin{array}{r} 2 \\ \times\ \ 1 \\ \hline \end{array}$$

11)
$$\begin{array}{r} 10 \\ \times\ \ 4 \\ \hline \end{array}$$

12)
$$\begin{array}{r} 6 \\ \times\ \ 3 \\ \hline \end{array}$$

13)
$$\begin{array}{r} 10 \\ \times\ \ 3 \\ \hline \end{array}$$

14)
$$\begin{array}{r} 6 \\ \times\ \ 4 \\ \hline \end{array}$$

15)
$$\begin{array}{r} 5 \\ \times\ \ 4 \\ \hline \end{array}$$

16)
$$\begin{array}{r} 4 \\ \times\ \ 5 \\ \hline \end{array}$$

17)
$$\begin{array}{r} 8 \\ \times\ \ 5 \\ \hline \end{array}$$

18)
$$\begin{array}{r} 3 \\ \times\ \ 4 \\ \hline \end{array}$$

19)
$$\begin{array}{r} 9 \\ \times\ \ 4 \\ \hline \end{array}$$

20)
$$\begin{array}{r} 6 \\ \times\ \ 2 \\ \hline \end{array}$$

21)
$$\begin{array}{r} 7 \\ \times\ \ 2 \\ \hline \end{array}$$

22)
$$\begin{array}{r} 10 \\ \times\ \ 2 \\ \hline \end{array}$$

23)
$$\begin{array}{r} 7 \\ \times\ \ 1 \\ \hline \end{array}$$

24)
$$\begin{array}{r} 9 \\ \times\ \ 5 \\ \hline \end{array}$$

25)
$$\begin{array}{r} 5 \\ \times\ \ 2 \\ \hline \end{array}$$

26)
$$\begin{array}{r} 1 \\ \times\ \ 1 \\ \hline \end{array}$$

27)
$$\begin{array}{r} 10 \\ \times\ \ 4 \\ \hline \end{array}$$

28)
$$\begin{array}{r} 1 \\ \times\ \ 2 \\ \hline \end{array}$$

29)
$$\begin{array}{r} 2 \\ \times\ \ 2 \\ \hline \end{array}$$

30)
$$\begin{array}{r} 10 \\ \times\ \ 3 \\ \hline \end{array}$$

Times Tables 6-10

1)
$$\begin{array}{r} 5 \\ \times\ 10 \\ \hline \end{array}$$

2)
$$\begin{array}{r} 4 \\ \times\ 8 \\ \hline \end{array}$$

3)
$$\begin{array}{r} 3 \\ \times\ 8 \\ \hline \end{array}$$

4)
$$\begin{array}{r} 7 \\ \times\ 7 \\ \hline \end{array}$$

5)
$$\begin{array}{r} 2 \\ \times\ 6 \\ \hline \end{array}$$

6)
$$\begin{array}{r} 3 \\ \times\ 9 \\ \hline \end{array}$$

7)
$$\begin{array}{r} 7 \\ \times\ 9 \\ \hline \end{array}$$

8)
$$\begin{array}{r} 6 \\ \times\ 10 \\ \hline \end{array}$$

9)
$$\begin{array}{r} 6 \\ \times\ 7 \\ \hline \end{array}$$

10)
$$\begin{array}{r} 5 \\ \times\ 8 \\ \hline \end{array}$$

11)
$$\begin{array}{r} 10 \\ \times\ 9 \\ \hline \end{array}$$

12)
$$\begin{array}{r} 1 \\ \times\ 8 \\ \hline \end{array}$$

13)
$$\begin{array}{r} 6 \\ \times\ 10 \\ \hline \end{array}$$

14)
$$\begin{array}{r} 5 \\ \times\ 8 \\ \hline \end{array}$$

15)
$$\begin{array}{r} 9 \\ \times\ 6 \\ \hline \end{array}$$

16)
$$\begin{array}{r} 1 \\ \times\ 9 \\ \hline \end{array}$$

17)
$$\begin{array}{r} 2 \\ \times\ 6 \\ \hline \end{array}$$

18)
$$\begin{array}{r} 4 \\ \times\ 10 \\ \hline \end{array}$$

19)
$$\begin{array}{r} 5 \\ \times\ 6 \\ \hline \end{array}$$

20)
$$\begin{array}{r} 1 \\ \times\ 8 \\ \hline \end{array}$$

21)
$$\begin{array}{r} 1 \\ \times\ 7 \\ \hline \end{array}$$

22)
$$\begin{array}{r} 10 \\ \times\ 7 \\ \hline \end{array}$$

23)
$$\begin{array}{r} 6 \\ \times\ 7 \\ \hline \end{array}$$

24)
$$\begin{array}{r} 3 \\ \times\ 7 \\ \hline \end{array}$$

25)
$$\begin{array}{r} 8 \\ \times\ 10 \\ \hline \end{array}$$

26)
$$\begin{array}{r} 9 \\ \times\ 8 \\ \hline \end{array}$$

27)
$$\begin{array}{r} 9 \\ \times\ 6 \\ \hline \end{array}$$

28)
$$\begin{array}{r} 8 \\ \times\ 7 \\ \hline \end{array}$$

29)
$$\begin{array}{r} 10 \\ \times\ 10 \\ \hline \end{array}$$

30)
$$\begin{array}{r} 4 \\ \times\ 8 \\ \hline \end{array}$$

1)
$$\begin{array}{r} 5 \\ \times\ 7 \\ \hline \end{array}$$

2)
$$\begin{array}{r} 2 \\ \times\ 8 \\ \hline \end{array}$$

3)
$$\begin{array}{r} 3 \\ \times\ 6 \\ \hline \end{array}$$

4)
$$\begin{array}{r} 4 \\ \times\ 6 \\ \hline \end{array}$$

5)
$$\begin{array}{r} 5 \\ \times\ 6 \\ \hline \end{array}$$

6)
$$\begin{array}{r} 5 \\ \times\ 9 \\ \hline \end{array}$$

7)
$$\begin{array}{r} 6 \\ \times\ 8 \\ \hline \end{array}$$

8)
$$\begin{array}{r} 10 \\ \times\ 7 \\ \hline \end{array}$$

9)
$$\begin{array}{r} 3 \\ \times\ 6 \\ \hline \end{array}$$

10)
$$\begin{array}{r} 2 \\ \times\ 9 \\ \hline \end{array}$$

11)
$$\begin{array}{r} 7 \\ \times\ 10 \\ \hline \end{array}$$

12)
$$\begin{array}{r} 8 \\ \times\ 8 \\ \hline \end{array}$$

13)
$$\begin{array}{r} 8 \\ \times\ 6 \\ \hline \end{array}$$

14)
$$\begin{array}{r} 5 \\ \times\ 6 \\ \hline \end{array}$$

15)
$$\begin{array}{r} 7 \\ \times\ 8 \\ \hline \end{array}$$

16)
$$\begin{array}{r} 9 \\ \times\ 9 \\ \hline \end{array}$$

17)
$$\begin{array}{r} 10 \\ \times\ 6 \\ \hline \end{array}$$

18)
$$\begin{array}{r} 2 \\ \times\ 10 \\ \hline \end{array}$$

19)
$$\begin{array}{r} 4 \\ \times\ 7 \\ \hline \end{array}$$

20)
$$\begin{array}{r} 3 \\ \times\ 8 \\ \hline \end{array}$$

21)
$$\begin{array}{r} 6 \\ \times\ 9 \\ \hline \end{array}$$

22)
$$\begin{array}{r} 7 \\ \times\ 9 \\ \hline \end{array}$$

23)
$$\begin{array}{r} 7 \\ \times\ 8 \\ \hline \end{array}$$

24)
$$\begin{array}{r} 9 \\ \times\ 7 \\ \hline \end{array}$$

25)
$$\begin{array}{r} 6 \\ \times\ 9 \\ \hline \end{array}$$

26)
$$\begin{array}{r} 1 \\ \times\ 7 \\ \hline \end{array}$$

27)
$$\begin{array}{r} 5 \\ \times\ 8 \\ \hline \end{array}$$

28)
$$\begin{array}{r} 2 \\ \times\ 7 \\ \hline \end{array}$$

29)
$$\begin{array}{r} 8 \\ \times\ 6 \\ \hline \end{array}$$

30)
$$\begin{array}{r} 4 \\ \times\ 10 \\ \hline \end{array}$$

1)
$$\begin{array}{r} 4 \\ \times\ 10 \\ \hline \end{array}$$

2)
$$\begin{array}{r} 10 \\ \times\ 6 \\ \hline \end{array}$$

3)
$$\begin{array}{r} 2 \\ \times\ 10 \\ \hline \end{array}$$

4)
$$\begin{array}{r} 6 \\ \times\ 8 \\ \hline \end{array}$$

5)
$$\begin{array}{r} 8 \\ \times\ 8 \\ \hline \end{array}$$

6)
$$\begin{array}{r} 8 \\ \times\ 9 \\ \hline \end{array}$$

7)
$$\begin{array}{r} 10 \\ \times\ 7 \\ \hline \end{array}$$

8)
$$\begin{array}{r} 7 \\ \times\ 6 \\ \hline \end{array}$$

9)
$$\begin{array}{r} 8 \\ \times\ 7 \\ \hline \end{array}$$

10)
$$\begin{array}{r} 1 \\ \times\ 7 \\ \hline \end{array}$$

11)
$$\begin{array}{r} 4 \\ \times\ 7 \\ \hline \end{array}$$

12)
$$\begin{array}{r} 4 \\ \times\ 7 \\ \hline \end{array}$$

13)
$$\begin{array}{r} 7 \\ \times\ 7 \\ \hline \end{array}$$

14)
$$\begin{array}{r} 3 \\ \times\ 6 \\ \hline \end{array}$$

15)
$$\begin{array}{r} 9 \\ \times\ 9 \\ \hline \end{array}$$

16)
$$\begin{array}{r} 7 \\ \times\ 10 \\ \hline \end{array}$$

17)
$$\begin{array}{r} 10 \\ \times\ 7 \\ \hline \end{array}$$

18)
$$\begin{array}{r} 10 \\ \times\ 7 \\ \hline \end{array}$$

19)
$$\begin{array}{r} 4 \\ \times\ 8 \\ \hline \end{array}$$

20)
$$\begin{array}{r} 10 \\ \times\ 10 \\ \hline \end{array}$$

21)
$$\begin{array}{r} 8 \\ \times\ 10 \\ \hline \end{array}$$

22)
$$\begin{array}{r} 7 \\ \times\ 10 \\ \hline \end{array}$$

23)
$$\begin{array}{r} 6 \\ \times\ 6 \\ \hline \end{array}$$

24)
$$\begin{array}{r} 1 \\ \times\ 6 \\ \hline \end{array}$$

25)
$$\begin{array}{r} 4 \\ \times\ 7 \\ \hline \end{array}$$

26)
$$\begin{array}{r} 5 \\ \times\ 7 \\ \hline \end{array}$$

27)
$$\begin{array}{r} 1 \\ \times\ 7 \\ \hline \end{array}$$

28)
$$\begin{array}{r} 7 \\ \times\ 8 \\ \hline \end{array}$$

29)
$$\begin{array}{r} 4 \\ \times\ 7 \\ \hline \end{array}$$

30)
$$\begin{array}{r} 3 \\ \times\ 10 \\ \hline \end{array}$$

1)
```
    10
×    7
─────
```

2)
```
     8
×    7
─────
```

3)
```
     4
×    6
─────
```

4)
```
     9
×    6
─────
```

5)
```
    10
×   10
─────
```

6)
```
     6
×    8
─────
```

7)
```
     3
×    7
─────
```

8)
```
     3
×    8
─────
```

9)
```
     1
×    6
─────
```

10)
```
    10
×   10
─────
```

11)
```
     1
×    7
─────
```

12)
```
     7
×    7
─────
```

13)
```
     6
×    7
─────
```

14)
```
     7
×    9
─────
```

15)
```
     5
×   10
─────
```

16)
```
     1
×    6
─────
```

17)
```
     1
×    9
─────
```

18)
```
     4
×    8
─────
```

19)
```
     5
×    7
─────
```

20)
```
     7
×    9
─────
```

21)
```
     8
×    7
─────
```

22)
```
     3
×    8
─────
```

23)
```
     7
×   10
─────
```

24)
```
     1
×    9
─────
```

25)
```
     5
×    7
─────
```

26)
```
     5
×    7
─────
```

27)
```
     9
×    7
─────
```

28)
```
     9
×    6
─────
```

29)
```
     4
×    9
─────
```

30)
```
     2
×   10
─────
```

1) 7 × 9

2) 3 × 9

3) 4 × 6

4) 6 × 10

5) 9 × 8

6) 4 × 8

7) 8 × 9

8) 2 × 8

9) 4 × 7

10) 4 × 7

11) 2 × 8

12) 1 × 8

13) 8 × 10

14) 1 × 9

15) 1 × 8

16) 6 × 9

17) 2 × 6

18) 6 × 8

19) 10 × 9

20) 9 × 8

21) 1 × 7

22) 3 × 7

23) 10 × 9

24) 1 × 7

25) 9 × 10

26) 5 × 8

27) 1 × 8

28) 3 × 8

29) 1 × 7

30) 6 × 9

1)
$$\begin{array}{r} 2 \\ \times\ 9 \\ \hline \end{array}$$

2)
$$\begin{array}{r} 5 \\ \times\ 8 \\ \hline \end{array}$$

3)
$$\begin{array}{r} 5 \\ \times\ 8 \\ \hline \end{array}$$

4)
$$\begin{array}{r} 3 \\ \times\ 7 \\ \hline \end{array}$$

5)
$$\begin{array}{r} 5 \\ \times\ 6 \\ \hline \end{array}$$

6)
$$\begin{array}{r} 3 \\ \times\ 6 \\ \hline \end{array}$$

7)
$$\begin{array}{r} 8 \\ \times\ 9 \\ \hline \end{array}$$

8)
$$\begin{array}{r} 7 \\ \times\ 6 \\ \hline \end{array}$$

9)
$$\begin{array}{r} 8 \\ \times\ 8 \\ \hline \end{array}$$

10)
$$\begin{array}{r} 5 \\ \times\ 10 \\ \hline \end{array}$$

11)
$$\begin{array}{r} 2 \\ \times\ 6 \\ \hline \end{array}$$

12)
$$\begin{array}{r} 7 \\ \times\ 7 \\ \hline \end{array}$$

13)
$$\begin{array}{r} 8 \\ \times\ 10 \\ \hline \end{array}$$

14)
$$\begin{array}{r} 3 \\ \times\ 9 \\ \hline \end{array}$$

15)
$$\begin{array}{r} 10 \\ \times\ 8 \\ \hline \end{array}$$

16)
$$\begin{array}{r} 1 \\ \times\ 8 \\ \hline \end{array}$$

17)
$$\begin{array}{r} 6 \\ \times\ 8 \\ \hline \end{array}$$

18)
$$\begin{array}{r} 4 \\ \times\ 8 \\ \hline \end{array}$$

19)
$$\begin{array}{r} 7 \\ \times\ 7 \\ \hline \end{array}$$

20)
$$\begin{array}{r} 3 \\ \times\ 7 \\ \hline \end{array}$$

21)
$$\begin{array}{r} 9 \\ \times\ 7 \\ \hline \end{array}$$

22)
$$\begin{array}{r} 7 \\ \times\ 6 \\ \hline \end{array}$$

23)
$$\begin{array}{r} 6 \\ \times\ 9 \\ \hline \end{array}$$

24)
$$\begin{array}{r} 6 \\ \times\ 9 \\ \hline \end{array}$$

25)
$$\begin{array}{r} 8 \\ \times\ 7 \\ \hline \end{array}$$

26)
$$\begin{array}{r} 3 \\ \times\ 6 \\ \hline \end{array}$$

27)
$$\begin{array}{r} 10 \\ \times\ 8 \\ \hline \end{array}$$

28)
$$\begin{array}{r} 6 \\ \times\ 7 \\ \hline \end{array}$$

29)
$$\begin{array}{r} 7 \\ \times\ 6 \\ \hline \end{array}$$

30)
$$\begin{array}{r} 10 \\ \times\ 7 \\ \hline \end{array}$$

1) 5 × 7

2) 1 × 6

3) 4 × 6

4) 6 × 8

5) 9 × 6

6) 7 × 8

7) 4 × 9

8) 3 × 9

9) 1 × 8

10) 8 × 7

11) 8 × 9

12) 4 × 8

13) 3 × 7

14) 7 × 10

15) 7 × 6

16) 1 × 10

17) 6 × 10

18) 10 × 7

19) 10 × 7

20) 3 × 8

21) 2 × 7

22) 8 × 10

23) 10 × 6

24) 3 × 8

25) 10 × 8

26) 1 × 8

27) 7 × 8

28) 4 × 6

29) 3 × 8

30) 3 × 6

1) 2 × 7

2) 4 × 8

3) 6 × 6

4) 9 × 8

5) 6 × 6

6) 3 × 7

7) 6 × 10

8) 7 × 9

9) 5 × 9

10) 6 × 9

11) 3 × 7

12) 8 × 6

13) 10 × 10

14) 4 × 8

15) 9 × 6

16) 6 × 9

17) 6 × 7

18) 8 × 7

19) 4 × 10

20) 3 × 10

21) 9 × 9

22) 8 × 7

23) 9 × 6

24) 1 × 10

25) 4 × 7

26) 4 × 7

27) 6 × 8

28) 2 × 6

29) 5 × 6

30) 10 × 7

Telling Time

Circle the answer
with the
correct time!

1)
(A) 6:25
(B) 1:20
(C) 4:10
(D) 5:05

2)
(A) 1:25
(B) 11:10
(C) 6:05
(D) 9:20

3)
(A) 3:10
(B) 11:05
(C) 6:20
(D) 10:25

4)
(A) 1:20
(B) 2:10
(C) 9:25
(D) 5:05

5)
(A) 3:05
(B) 11:25
(C) 1:10
(D) 10:20

6)
(A) 3:20
(B) 11:05
(C) 6:25
(D) 4:10

7)
(A) 7:05
(B) 4:20
(C) 10:10
(D) 6:25

8)
(A) 7:05
(B) 1:10
(C) 8:25
(D) 10:20

9)
(A) 1:05
(B) 7:10
(C) 8:25
(D) 11:20

1)
- (A) 6:25
- (B) 1:20
- (C) 8:05
- (D) 5:10

2)
- (A) 10:05
- (B) 8:10
- (C) 11:20
- (D) 2:25

3)
- (A) 2:20
- (B) 1:10
- (C) 8:05
- (D) 10:25

4)
- (A) 6:05
- (B) 5:20
- (C) 1:25
- (D) 11:10

5)
- (A) 6:05
- (B) 9:25
- (C) 5:10
- (D) 3:20

6)
- (A) 10:05
- (B) 8:20
- (C) 11:10
- (D) 9:25

7)
- (A) 8:10
- (B) 7:25
- (C) 4:05
- (D) 1:20

8)
- (A) 4:05
- (B) 8:25
- (C) 3:20
- (D) 2:10

9)
- (A) 1:10
- (B) 4:25
- (C) 10:05
- (D) 8:20

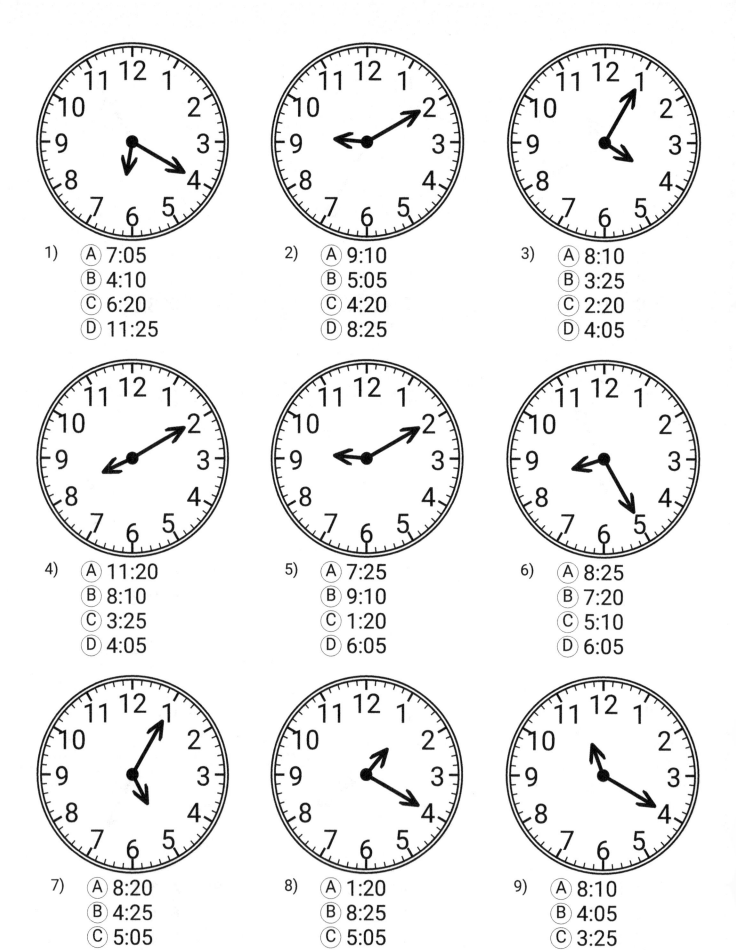

1)
(A) 7:05
(B) 4:10
(C) 6:20
(D) 11:25

2)
(A) 9:10
(B) 5:05
(C) 4:20
(D) 8:25

3)
(A) 8:10
(B) 3:25
(C) 2:20
(D) 4:05

4)
(A) 11:20
(B) 8:10
(C) 3:25
(D) 4:05

5)
(A) 7:25
(B) 9:10
(C) 1:20
(D) 6:05

6)
(A) 8:25
(B) 7:20
(C) 5:10
(D) 6:05

7)
(A) 8:20
(B) 4:25
(C) 5:05
(D) 6:10

8)
(A) 1:20
(B) 8:25
(C) 5:05
(D) 2:10

9)
(A) 8:10
(B) 4:05
(C) 3:25
(D) 11:20

Page 62

1)
Ⓐ 3:20
Ⓑ 8:25
Ⓒ 5:05
Ⓓ 1:10

2)
Ⓐ 9:10
Ⓑ 3:25
Ⓒ 2:20
Ⓓ 8:05

3)
Ⓐ 10:20
Ⓑ 4:25
Ⓒ 6:10
Ⓓ 9:05

4)
Ⓐ 7:05
Ⓑ 10:10
Ⓒ 11:25
Ⓓ 2:20

5)
Ⓐ 4:20
Ⓑ 8:10
Ⓒ 10:25
Ⓓ 3:05

6)
Ⓐ 9:25
Ⓑ 11:20
Ⓒ 4:10
Ⓓ 10:05

7)
Ⓐ 1:20
Ⓑ 10:10
Ⓒ 6:05
Ⓓ 5:25

8)
Ⓐ 7:10
Ⓑ 6:25
Ⓒ 4:20
Ⓓ 1:05

9)
Ⓐ 1:10
Ⓑ 7:05
Ⓒ 6:25
Ⓓ 10:20

1) Ⓐ 5:10
     Ⓑ 9:20
     Ⓒ 6:05
     Ⓓ 2:25

2) Ⓐ 2:10
     Ⓑ 11:05
     Ⓒ 3:20
     Ⓓ 4:25

3) Ⓐ 11:20
     Ⓑ 10:05
     Ⓒ 3:25
     Ⓓ 4:10

4) Ⓐ 10:25
     Ⓑ 6:05
     Ⓒ 2:10
     Ⓓ 8:20

5) Ⓐ 10:05
     Ⓑ 2:25
     Ⓒ 4:20
     Ⓓ 1:10

6) Ⓐ 10:05
     Ⓑ 6:10
     Ⓒ 11:20
     Ⓓ 4:25

7) Ⓐ 2:20
     Ⓑ 11:10
     Ⓒ 8:05
     Ⓓ 6:25

8) Ⓐ 10:05
     Ⓑ 8:10
     Ⓒ 6:25
     Ⓓ 11:20

9) Ⓐ 9:10
     Ⓑ 2:20
     Ⓒ 8:25
     Ⓓ 10:05

1)
Ⓐ 5:05
Ⓑ 1:20
Ⓒ 11:25
Ⓓ 7:10

2)
Ⓐ 1:05
Ⓑ 4:10
Ⓒ 9:25
Ⓓ 2:20

3)
Ⓐ 10:25
Ⓑ 6:10
Ⓒ 8:05
Ⓓ 2:20

4)
Ⓐ 8:20
Ⓑ 9:25
Ⓒ 11:10
Ⓓ 3:05

5)
Ⓐ 11:20
Ⓑ 2:10
Ⓒ 4:25
Ⓓ 9:05

6)
Ⓐ 8:20
Ⓑ 1:05
Ⓒ 9:10
Ⓓ 4:25

7)
Ⓐ 7:20
Ⓑ 11:10
Ⓒ 6:05
Ⓓ 10:25

8)
Ⓐ 10:20
Ⓑ 8:10
Ⓒ 1:05
Ⓓ 6:25

9)
Ⓐ 6:25
Ⓑ 4:20
Ⓒ 9:10
Ⓓ 7:05

1)
   Ⓐ 1:25
   Ⓑ 4:20
   Ⓒ 10:10
   Ⓓ 6:05

2)
   Ⓐ 6:05
   Ⓑ 1:25
   Ⓒ 9:10
   Ⓓ 10:20

3)
   Ⓐ 1:10
   Ⓑ 10:05
   Ⓒ 7:20
   Ⓓ 9:25

4)
   Ⓐ 6:25
   Ⓑ 7:05
   Ⓒ 1:10
   Ⓓ 4:20

5)
   Ⓐ 7:10
   Ⓑ 4:05
   Ⓒ 9:25
   Ⓓ 11:20

6)
   Ⓐ 8:20
   Ⓑ 10:05
   Ⓒ 1:10
   Ⓓ 5:25

7)
   Ⓐ 8:05
   Ⓑ 6:20
   Ⓒ 3:25
   Ⓓ 2:10

8)
   Ⓐ 2:10
   Ⓑ 3:05
   Ⓒ 6:20
   Ⓓ 7:25

9)
   Ⓐ 2:20
   Ⓑ 6:05
   Ⓒ 4:10
   Ⓓ 7:25

1)
(A) 3:10
(B) 7:05
(C) 9:25
(D) 4:20

2)
(A) 6:20
(B) 2:25
(C) 1:10
(D) 9:05

3)
(A) 11:20
(B) 7:10
(C) 6:25
(D) 9:05

4)
(A) 6:05
(B) 4:25
(C) 7:10
(D) 1:20

5)
(A) 3:05
(B) 6:10
(C) 5:25
(D) 1:20

6)
(A) 11:25
(B) 3:20
(C) 2:05
(D) 1:10

7)
(A) 8:05
(B) 5:20
(C) 9:25
(D) 4:10

8)
(A) 4:25
(B) 11:05
(C) 6:10
(D) 7:20

9)
(A) 5:25
(B) 3:05
(C) 11:10
(D) 10:20

Telling Time

Write the correct time below each clock!

1) 3 : 20

2) 3 : 25

3) 7 : 20

4) 8 : 05

5) 10 : 10

6) 5 : 05

7) 10 : 20

8) 11 : 05

9) 1 : 25

10) 8 : 10

11) 5 : 25

12) 8 : 25

1) 5 : 20

2) 5 : 20

3) 8 : 25

4) 3 : 20

5) 4 : 10

6) 8 : 25

7) 10 : 05

8) 1 : 25

9) 5 : 05

10) 11 : 25

11) 11 : 20

12) 10 : 05

1) 10 : 25

2) 8 : 05

3) 3 : 10

4) 7 : 10

5) 1 : 10

6) 1 : 05

7) 2 : 10

8) 8 : 20

9) 1 : 10

10) 10 : 20

11) 1 : 20

12) 6 : 05

1)   6 : 25

2)   4 : 25

3)   4 : 20

4)   11 : 05

5)   1 : 25

6)   8 : 10

7)   10 : 25

8)   11 : 05

9)   4 : 20

10)   4 : 10

11)   1 : 25

12)   10 : 25

1)   7 : 10

2)   2 : 10

3)   8 : 25

4)   10 : 25

5)   10 : 25

6)   1 : 10

7)   11 : 10

8)   11 : 20

9)   4 : 05

10)   1 : 05

11)   9 : 25

12)   2 : 05

1) 3 : 10

2) 9 : 10

3) 6 : 25

4) 8 : 20

5) 8 : 05

6) 5 : 10

7) 3 : 05

8) 6 : 10

9) 6 : 10

10) 11 : 25

11) 11 : 05

12) 11 : 10

Page 74

1) 10 : 05

2) 9 : 25

3) 7 : 05

4) 3 : 20

5) 10 : 20

6) 7 : 25

7) 4 : 10

8) 7 : 05

9) 11 : 10

10) 10 : 20

11) 9 : 25

12) 3 : 20

1) 11 : 10

2) 8 : 25

3) 7 : 10

4) 8 : 05

5) 3 : 05

6) 6 : 25

7) 6 : 10

8) 2 : 10

9) 5 : 20

10) 2 : 10

11) 5 : 25

12) 9 : 05

Drawing Fractions

Color in the
shapes to reflect
the correct
fraction!

1) $\dfrac{4}{5}$ =

2) $\dfrac{3}{4}$ =

3) $\dfrac{1}{10}$ =

4) $\dfrac{2}{8}$ =

5) $\dfrac{2}{9}$ =

6) $\dfrac{3}{7}$ =

7) $\dfrac{4}{6}$ =

8) $\dfrac{1}{10}$ =

9) $\dfrac{3}{8}$ =

10) $\dfrac{2}{9}$ =

11) $\dfrac{1}{4}$ =

12) $\dfrac{1}{6}$ =

13) $\dfrac{1}{5}$ =

14) $\dfrac{4}{7}$ =

15) $\dfrac{3}{8}$ =

16) $\dfrac{2}{10}$ =

17) $\dfrac{1}{7}$ =

18) $\dfrac{3}{9}$ =

19) $\dfrac{4}{6}$ =

20) $\dfrac{2}{4}$ =

21) $\dfrac{4}{5}$ =

1) $\dfrac{1}{7}$ =

2) $\dfrac{4}{8}$ =

3) $\dfrac{2}{5}$ =

4) $\dfrac{3}{10}$ =

5) $\dfrac{4}{6}$ =

6) $\dfrac{3}{9}$ =

7) $\dfrac{2}{4}$ =

8) $\dfrac{1}{5}$ =

9) $\dfrac{1}{4}$ =

10) $\dfrac{2}{9}$ =

11) $\dfrac{4}{7}$ =

12) $\dfrac{3}{10}$ =

13) $\dfrac{2}{6}$ =

14) $\dfrac{4}{8}$ =

15) $\dfrac{1}{10}$ =

16) $\dfrac{3}{9}$ =

17) $\dfrac{2}{6}$ =

18) $\dfrac{4}{5}$ =

19) $\dfrac{1}{4}$ =

20) $\dfrac{3}{7}$ =

21) $\dfrac{4}{8}$ =

1)
$$\frac{3}{4} =$$

2)
$$\frac{4}{9} =$$

3)
$$\frac{2}{10} =$$

4)
$$\frac{1}{7} =$$

5)
$$\frac{2}{8} =$$

6)
$$\frac{3}{6} =$$

7)
$$\frac{4}{5} =$$

8)
$$\frac{1}{7} =$$

9)
$$\frac{1}{4} =$$

10)
$$\frac{1}{8} =$$

11)
$$\frac{3}{5} =$$

12)
$$\frac{2}{6} =$$

13)
$$\frac{3}{9} =$$

14)
$$\frac{4}{10} =$$

15)
$$\frac{1}{10} =$$

16)
$$\frac{2}{5} =$$

17)
$$\frac{3}{4} =$$

18)
$$\frac{1}{6} =$$

19)
$$\frac{4}{8} =$$

20)
$$\frac{2}{9} =$$

21)
$$\frac{1}{7} =$$

1)
$$\frac{4}{7} =$$

2)
$$\frac{2}{6} =$$

3)
$$\frac{3}{8} =$$

4)
$$\frac{1}{5} =$$

5)
$$\frac{1}{9} =$$

6)
$$\frac{2}{10} =$$

7)
$$\frac{3}{4} =$$

8)
$$\frac{1}{4} =$$

9)
$$\frac{1}{8} =$$

10)
$$\frac{3}{6} =$$

11)
$$\frac{2}{9} =$$

12)
$$\frac{4}{5} =$$

13)
$$\frac{3}{7} =$$

14)
$$\frac{1}{10} =$$

15)
$$\frac{4}{9} =$$

16)
$$\frac{2}{5} =$$

17)
$$\frac{4}{10} =$$

18)
$$\frac{2}{8} =$$

19)
$$\frac{3}{6} =$$

20)
$$\frac{1}{4} =$$

21)
$$\frac{2}{7} =$$

1) $\dfrac{4}{5}$ =

2) $\dfrac{3}{4}$ =

3) $\dfrac{2}{6}$ =

4) $\dfrac{1}{9}$ =

5) $\dfrac{3}{7}$ =

6) $\dfrac{4}{8}$ =

7) $\dfrac{1}{10}$ =

8) $\dfrac{2}{6}$ =

9) $\dfrac{2}{8}$ =

10) $\dfrac{3}{10}$ =

11) $\dfrac{1}{4}$ =

12) $\dfrac{1}{9}$ =

13) $\dfrac{3}{5}$ =

14) $\dfrac{1}{7}$ =

15) $\dfrac{2}{5}$ =

16) $\dfrac{4}{10}$ =

17) $\dfrac{3}{4}$ =

18) $\dfrac{4}{7}$ =

19) $\dfrac{1}{8}$ =

20) $\dfrac{2}{9}$ =

21) $\dfrac{4}{6}$ =

1) $\dfrac{3}{5}$ =

2) $\dfrac{2}{6}$ =

3) $\dfrac{4}{7}$ =

4) $\dfrac{1}{4}$ =

5) $\dfrac{2}{9}$ =

6) $\dfrac{4}{8}$ =

7) $\dfrac{3}{10}$ =

8) $\dfrac{1}{10}$ =

9) $\dfrac{3}{4}$ =

10) $\dfrac{4}{8}$ =

11) $\dfrac{1}{7}$ =

12) $\dfrac{2}{6}$ =

13) $\dfrac{4}{5}$ =

14) $\dfrac{3}{9}$ =

15) $\dfrac{1}{7}$ =

16) $\dfrac{2}{9}$ =

17) $\dfrac{1}{6}$ =

18) $\dfrac{3}{10}$ =

19) $\dfrac{1}{4}$ =

20) $\dfrac{2}{5}$ =

21) $\dfrac{2}{8}$ =

1) $\dfrac{1}{4} =$

2) $\dfrac{1}{8} =$

3) $\dfrac{2}{9} =$

4) $\dfrac{3}{7} =$

5) $\dfrac{3}{5} =$

6) $\dfrac{4}{6} =$

7) $\dfrac{1}{10} =$

8) $\dfrac{2}{7} =$

9) $\dfrac{3}{4} =$

10) $\dfrac{1}{6} =$

11) $\dfrac{4}{8} =$

12) $\dfrac{2}{10} =$

13) $\dfrac{2}{5} =$

14) $\dfrac{3}{9} =$

15) $\dfrac{1}{8} =$

16) $\dfrac{4}{5} =$

17) $\dfrac{4}{6} =$

18) $\dfrac{2}{9} =$

19) $\dfrac{3}{7} =$

20) $\dfrac{1}{10} =$

21) $\dfrac{3}{4} =$

Writing Fractions

Observe the shapes and write the shaded parts as a fraction of the whole!

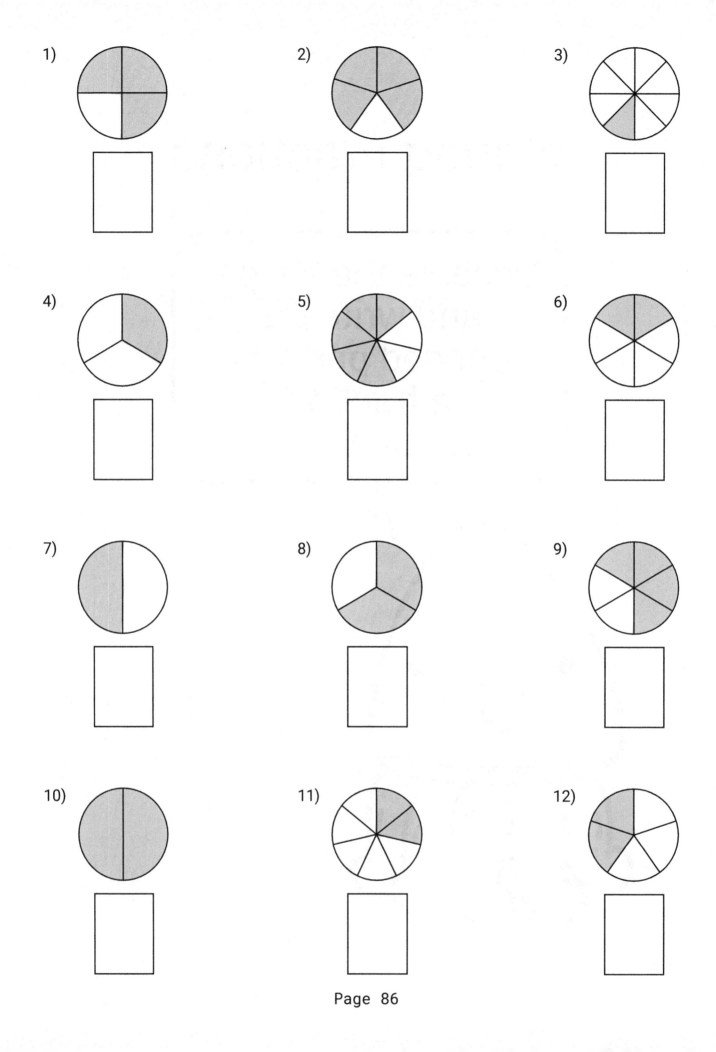

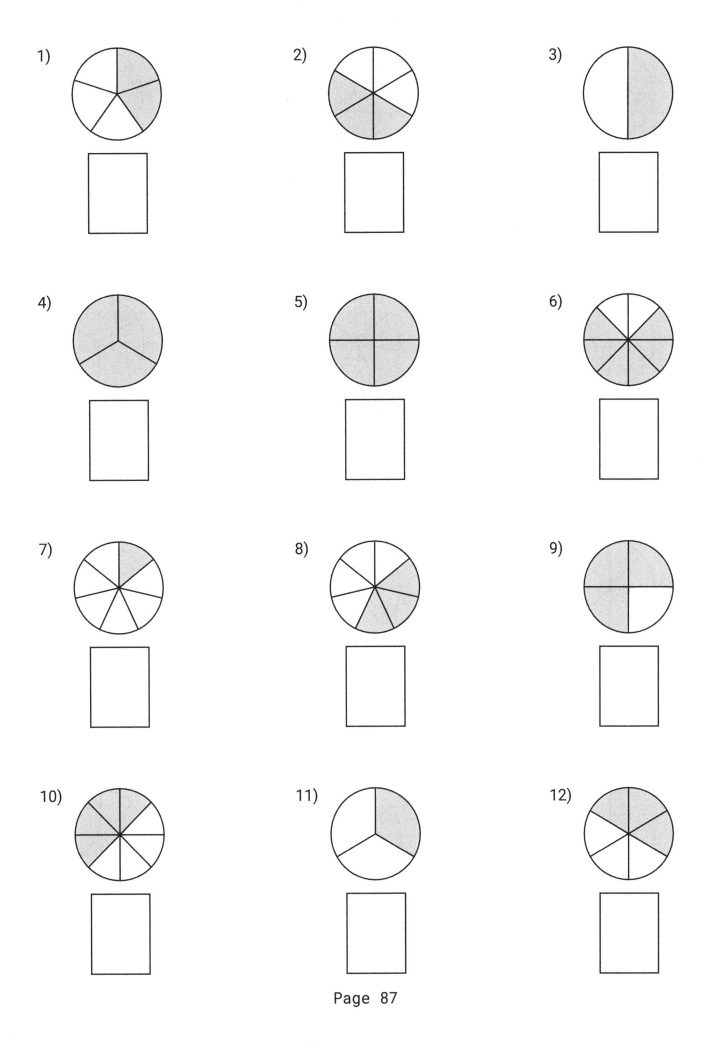

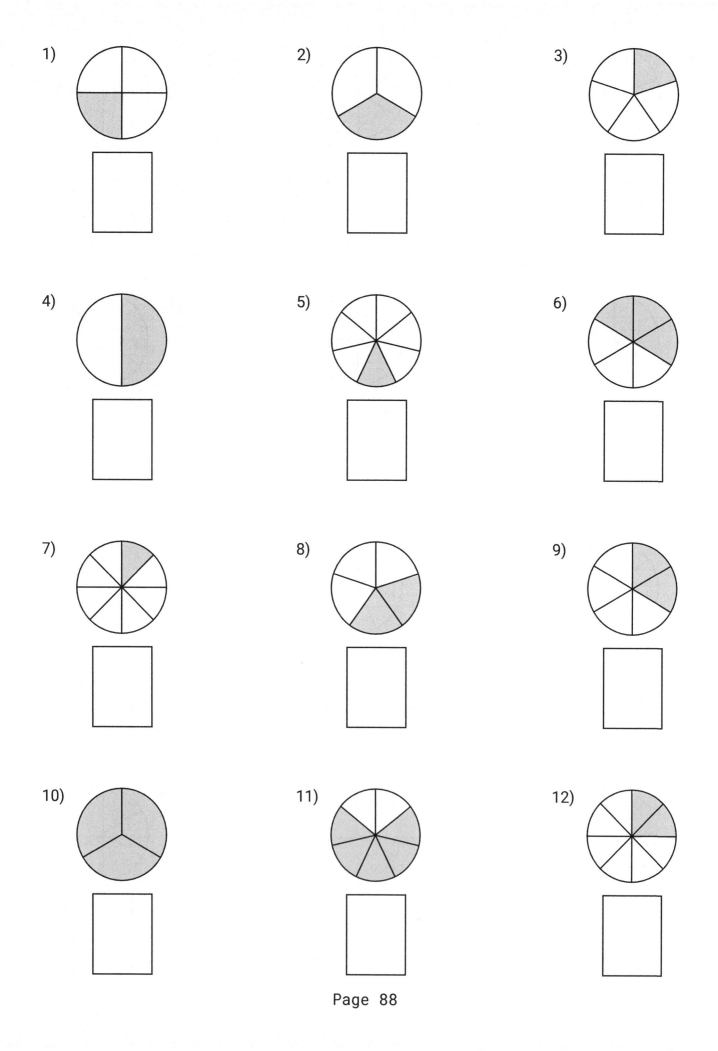

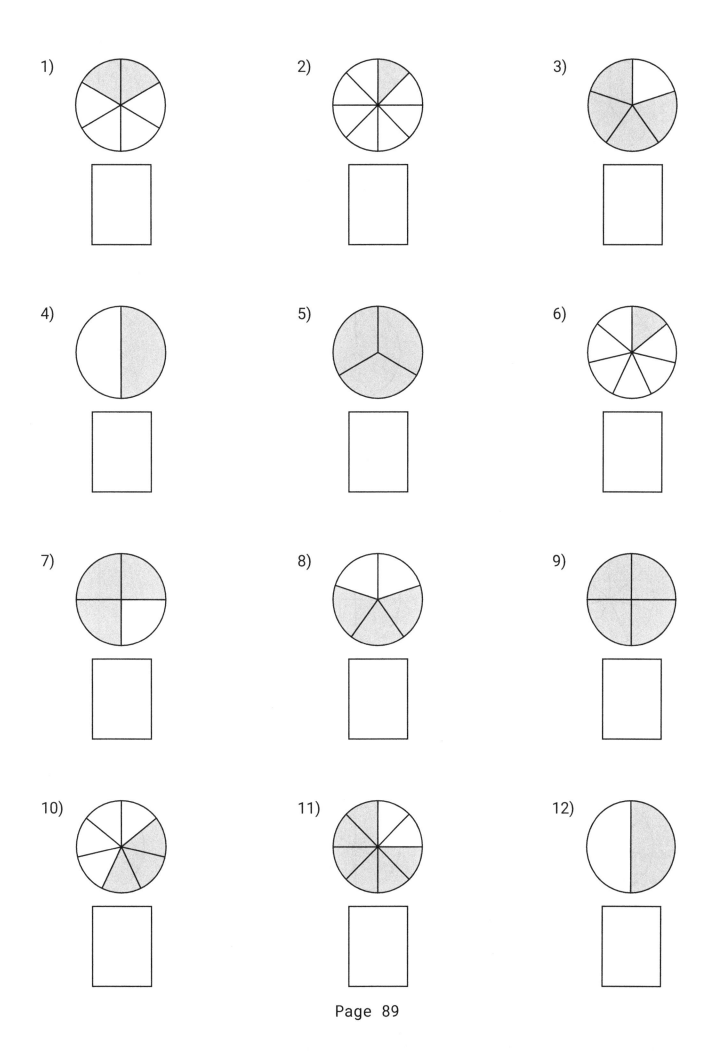

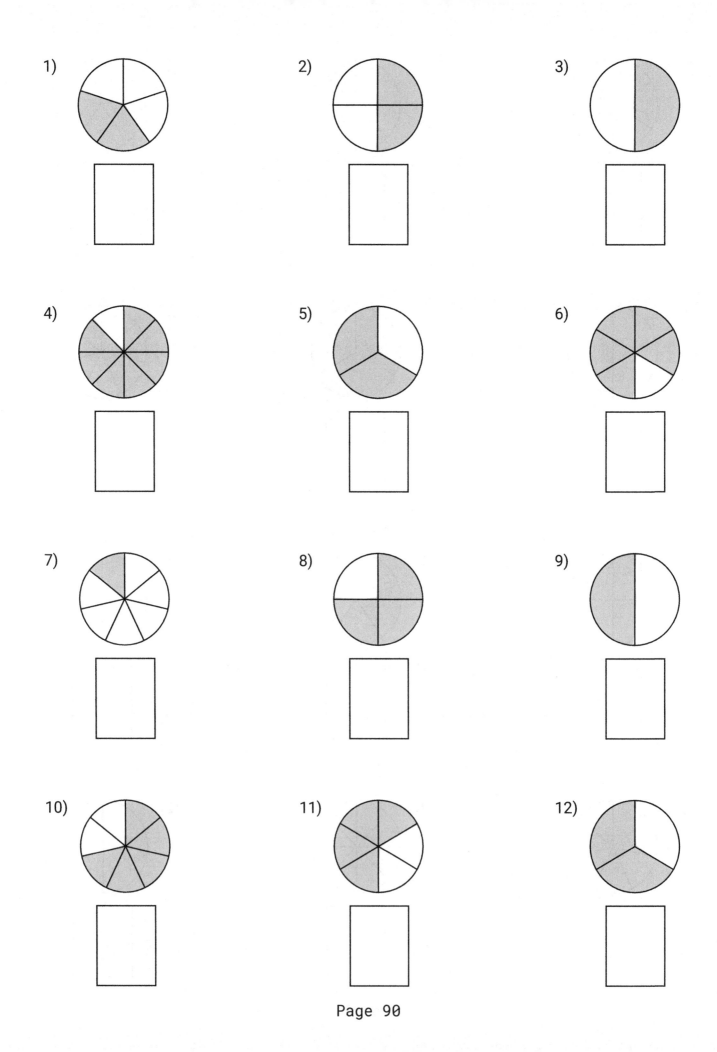

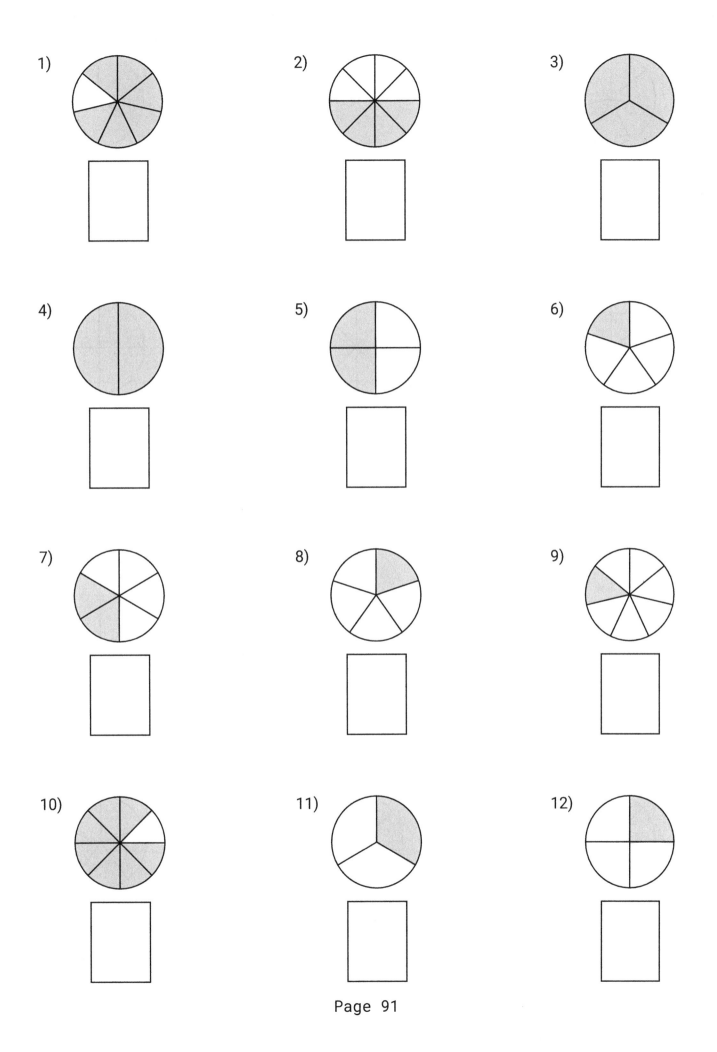

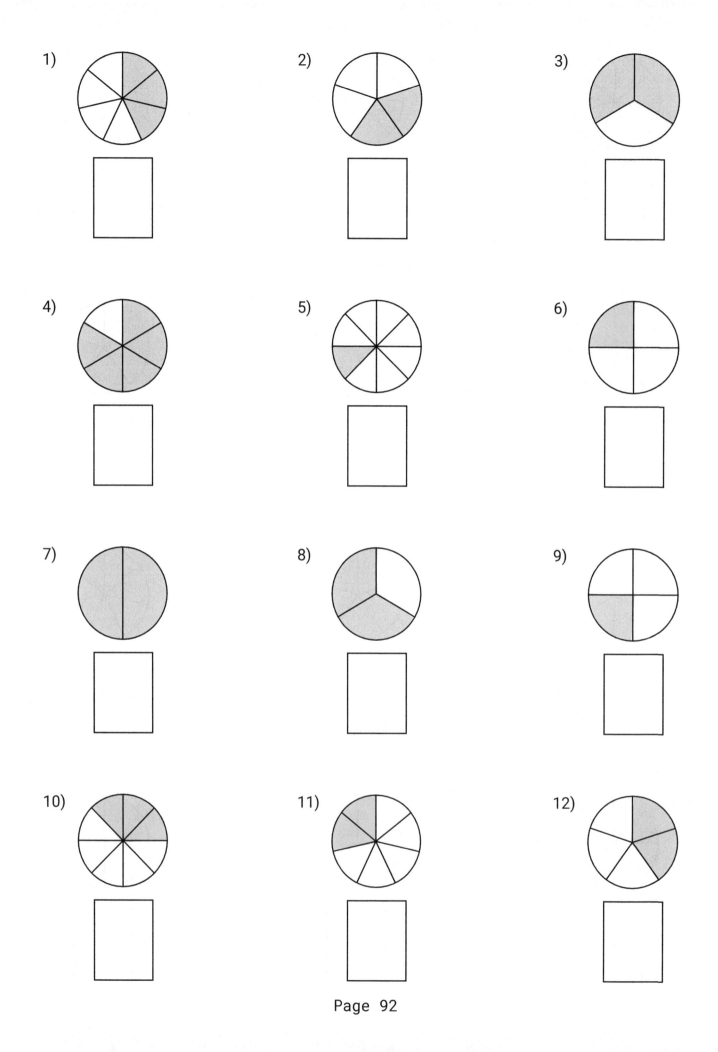

Additional recommended workbooks for future 2nd graders:

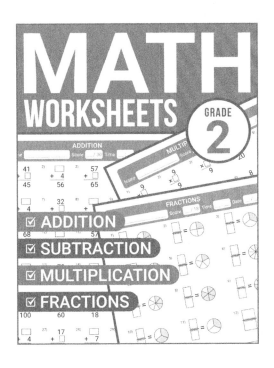

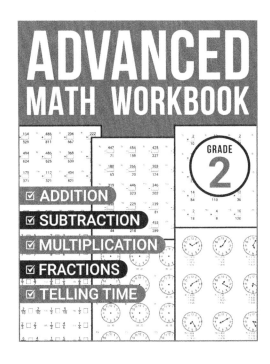

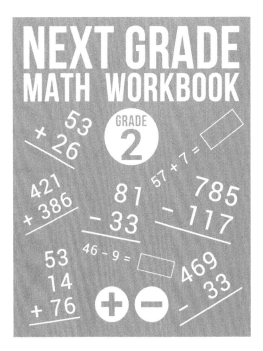

www.nermilio.com

Answer Key

Page 6, Item 1:
(1)94 (2)105 (3)51 (4)33 (5)24 (6)49 (7)24 (8)85 (9)55 (10)58 (11)64 (12)91 (13)67 (14)40 (15)73 (16)79 (17)106 (18)23 (19)84 (20)56 (21)47 (22)69 (23)103 (24)69 (25)103 (26)55 (27)27 (28)77 (29)59 (30)28

Page 7, Item 1:
(1)102 (2)75 (3)12 (4)100 (5)30 (6)84 (7)23 (8)28 (9)70 (10)15 (11)83 (12)101 (13)53 (14)81 (15)43 (16)96 (17)86 (18)25 (19)70 (20)89 (21)24 (22)28 (23)35 (24)106 (25)22 (26)34 (27)103 (28)88 (29)82 (30)66

Page 8, Item 1:
(1)80 (2)29 (3)29 (4)63 (5)63 (6)104 (7)70 (8)77 (9)95 (10)83 (11)21 (12)21 (13)27 (14)63 (15)97 (16)102 (17)35 (18)50 (19)48 (20)39 (21)55 (22)51 (23)64 (24)18 (25)18 (26)59 (27)92 (28)93 (29)28 (30)54

Page 9, Item 1:
(1)105 (2)38 (3)43 (4)29 (5)21 (6)44 (7)42 (8)28 (9)40 (10)75 (11)63 (12)59 (13)41 (14)66 (15)40 (16)79 (17)15 (18)45 (19)37 (20)36 (21)60 (22)22 (23)30 (24)90 (25)34 (26)49 (27)81 (28)95 (29)90 (30)42

Page 10, Item 1:
(1)26 (2)36 (3)73 (4)33 (5)15 (6)38 (7)85 (8)79 (9)91 (10)90 (11)88 (12)69 (13)17 (14)78 (15)11 (16)56 (17)88 (18)71 (19)84 (20)69 (21)33 (22)45 (23)84 (24)87 (25)94 (26)77 (27)78 (28)18 (29)77 (30)48

Page 11, Item 1:
(1)86 (2)24 (3)93 (4)82 (5)69 (6)95 (7)43 (8)36 (9)90 (10)35 (11)72 (12)32 (13)48 (14)58 (15)50 (16)45 (17)58 (18)27 (19)59 (20)33 (21)39 (22)73 (23)74 (24)68 (25)102 (26)96 (27)107 (28)43 (29)23 (30)19

Page 12, Item 1:
(1)42 (2)54 (3)47 (4)85 (5)94 (6)21 (7)17 (8)107 (9)32 (10)27 (11)23 (12)88 (13)70 (14)20 (15)56 (16)81 (17)71 (18)42 (19)36 (20)98 (21)74 (22)63 (23)90 (24)42 (25)48 (26)49 (27)27 (28)50 (29)40 (30)69

Page 13, Item 1:
(1)25 (2)38 (3)54 (4)71 (5)95 (6)49 (7)34 (8)53 (9)24 (10)43 (11)62 (12)17 (13)103 (14)42 (15)74 (16)55 (17)83 (18)103 (19)31 (20)69 (21)66 (22)51 (23)68 (24)25 (25)76 (26)105 (27)19 (28)46 (29)93 (30)97

Page 15, Item 1:
(1)62 (2)96 (3)156 (4)160 (5)82 (6)131 (7)105 (8)90 (9)178 (10)81 (11)141 (12)88 (13)125 (14)180 (15)155 (16)85 (17)64 (18)84 (19)124 (20)126 (21)116 (22)83 (23)115 (24)145 (25)75 (26)133 (27)151 (28)97 (29)121 (30)111

Page 16, Item 1:
(1)113 (2)106 (3)87 (4)77 (5)103 (6)76 (7)72 (8)98 (9)112 (10)152 (11)65 (12)53 (13)74 (14)60 (15)41 (16)143 (17)37 (18)138 (19)153 (20)88 (21)127 (22)119 (23)105 (24)85 (25)152 (26)87 (27)175 (28)191 (29)89 (30)104

Page 17, Item 1:
(1)45 (2)121 (3)126 (4)90 (5)168 (6)159 (7)54 (8)65 (9)143 (10)146 (11)141 (12)113 (13)104 (14)81 (15)128 (16)147 (17)55 (18)173 (19)141 (20)116 (21)138 (22)94 (23)97 (24)123 (25)107 (26)106 (27)69 (28)75 (29)98 (30)132

Page 18, Item 1:
(1)147 (2)90 (3)143 (4)141 (5)139 (6)101 (7)58 (8)192 (9)46 (10)106 (11)47 (12)120 (13)163 (14)90 (15)126 (16)68 (17)41 (18)118 (19)98 (20)140 (21)171 (22)124 (23)124 (24)156 (25)125 (26)88 (27)127 (28)67 (29)165 (30)127

Page 19, Item 1:
(1)82 (2)102 (3)174 (4)115 (5)121 (6)53 (7)93 (8)56 (9)153 (10)59 (11)62 (12)170 (13)65 (14)103 (15)72 (16)83 (17)150 (18)85 (19)113 (20)73 (21)150 (22)158 (23)152 (24)128 (25)141 (26)122 (27)59 (28)152 (29)98 (30)98

Page 20, Item 1:
(1)120 (2)125 (3)75 (4)108 (5)125 (6)118 (7)162 (8)71 (9)151 (10)110 (11)71 (12)77 (13)116 (14)113 (15)119 (16)90 (17)101 (18)149 (19)55 (20)115 (21)68 (22)155 (23)133 (24)190 (25)138 (26)115 (27)186 (28)71 (29)60 (30)123

Page 21, Item 1:
(1)76 (2)83 (3)68 (4)172 (5)84 (6)113 (7)112 (8)158 (9)82 (10)197 (11)176 (12)121 (13)153 (14)135 (15)56 (16)156 (17)109 (18)154 (19)85 (20)133 (21)90 (22)61 (23)106 (24)99 (25)142 (26)89 (27)131 (28)107 (29)171 (30)130

Page 22, Item 1:
(1)110 (2)86 (3)60 (4)141 (5)93 (6)118 (7)77 (8)45 (9)75 (10)112 (11)109 (12)67 (13)115 (14)141 (15)78 (16)53 (17)140 (18)134 (19)139 (20)46 (21)79 (22)117 (23)136 (24)146 (25)99 (26)133 (27)41 (28)93 (29)116 (30)71

Page 24, Item 1:
(1)13 (2)71 (3)69 (4)31 (5)22 (6)7 (7)30 (8)59 (9)70 (10)14 (11)47 (12)40 (13)39 (14)34 (15)76 (16)49 (17)16 (18)64 (19)77 (20)81 (21)40 (22)93 (23)14 (24)27 (25)93 (26)70 (27)26 (28)12 (29)15 (30)58

Page 25, Item 1:
(1)33 (2)58 (3)95 (4)31 (5)36 (6)9 (7)10 (8)80 (9)55 (10)60 (11)42 (12)44 (13)97 (14)27 (15)56 (16)46 (17)69 (18)48 (19)20 (20)7 (21)43 (22)57 (23)76 (24)38 (25)64 (26)68 (27)25 (28)10 (29)68 (30)22

Page 26, Item 1:
(1)25 (2)42 (3)92 (4)19 (5)41 (6)53 (7)75 (8)78 (9)26 (10)17 (11)79 (12)70 (13)72 (14)27 (15)55 (16)50 (17)61 (18)84 (19)93 (20)50 (21)68 (22)56 (23)52 (24)17 (25)13 (26)96 (27)26 (28)45 (29)66 (30)92

Page 27, Item 1:
(1)48 (2)57 (3)98 (4)25 (5)73 (6)86 (7)58 (8)68 (9)44 (10)81 (11)4 (12)84 (13)43 (14)76 (15)74 (16)50 (17)74 (18)15 (19)10 (20)85 (21)15 (22)64 (23)28 (24)84 (25)80 (26)90 (27)61 (28)91 (29)65 (30)63

Page 28, Item 1:
(1)66 (2)97 (3)91 (4)41 (5)7 (6)61 (7)76
(8)97 (9)67 (10)19 (11)67 (12)54 (13)31
(14)8 (15)86 (16)63 (17)35 (18)25 (19)15
(20)50 (21)30 (22)66 (23)16 (24)74 (25)39
(26)24 (27)49 (28)72 (29)26 (30)87

Page 29, Item 1:
(1)10 (2)9 (3)25 (4)28 (5)49 (6)11 (7)71
(8)72 (9)35 (10)53 (11)67 (12)92 (13)53
(14)77 (15)32 (16)53 (17)22 (18)6 (19)26
(20)52 (21)13 (22)37 (23)79 (24)33 (25)81
(26)55 (27)51 (28)65 (29)77 (30)8

Page 30, Item 1:
(1)34 (2)66 (3)37 (4)94 (5)69 (6)72 (7)90
(8)48 (9)45 (10)32 (11)9 (12)20 (13)13
(14)68 (15)66 (16)39 (17)37 (18)83 (19)58
(20)12 (21)8 (22)90 (23)64 (24)70 (25)14
(26)61 (27)22 (28)89 (29)41 (30)25

Page 31, Item 1:
(1)34 (2)4 (3)6 (4)58 (5)42 (6)52 (7)32
(8)11 (9)24 (10)32 (11)67 (12)80 (13)58
(14)26 (15)45 (16)32 (17)17 (18)82 (19)22
(20)94 (21)93 (22)25 (23)45 (24)37 (25)14
(26)91 (27)31 (28)65 (29)34 (30)15

Page 33, Item 1:
(1)53 (2)22 (3)0 (4)19 (5)0 (6)8 (7)31 (8)10
(9)11 (10)23 (11)58 (12)65 (13)21 (14)27
(15)35 (16)51 (17)16 (18)0 (19)36 (20)29
(21)28 (22)56 (23)31 (24)16 (25)32 (26)14
(27)1 (28)31 (29)24 (30)29

Page 34, Item 1:
(1)23 (2)45 (3)79 (4)38 (5)44 (6)10 (7)14
(8)30 (9)28 (10)32 (11)56 (12)50 (13)15
(14)29 (15)55 (16)3 (17)75 (18)26 (19)65
(20)29 (21)10 (22)30 (23)37 (24)41 (25)23
(26)2 (27)42 (28)54 (29)26 (30)48

Page 35, Item 1:
(1)39 (2)25 (3)7 (4)18 (5)15 (6)32 (7)28

(8)29 (9)4 (10)39 (11)62 (12)5 (13)81
(14)65 (15)20 (16)12 (17)3 (18)3 (19)29
(20)73 (21)36 (22)27 (23)46 (24)8 (25)16
(26)62 (27)12 (28)51 (29)51 (30)29

Page 36, Item 1:
(1)11 (2)24 (3)34 (4)25 (5)10 (6)46 (7)6
(8)47 (9)1 (10)49 (11)37 (12)73 (13)12
(14)23 (15)57 (16)47 (17)14 (18)40 (19)55
(20)78 (21)15 (22)24 (23)2 (24)64 (25)29
(26)10 (27)25 (28)72 (29)43 (30)41

Page 37, Item 1:
(1)10 (2)20 (3)51 (4)18 (5)45 (6)0 (7)14
(8)14 (9)15 (10)49 (11)62 (12)63 (13)36
(14)1 (15)58 (16)63 (17)36 (18)1 (19)0
(20)21 (21)29 (22)26 (23)20 (24)34 (25)47
(26)27 (27)13 (28)24 (29)20 (30)16

Page 38, Item 1:
(1)9 (2)14 (3)14 (4)51 (5)74 (6)67 (7)4 (8)2
(9)34 (10)31 (11)55 (12)6 (13)34 (14)46
(15)42 (16)18 (17)22 (18)30 (19)52 (20)7
(21)68 (22)40 (23)41 (24)3 (25)29 (26)26
(27)5 (28)53 (29)12 (30)26

Page 39, Item 1:
(1)53 (2)8 (3)1 (4)20 (5)13 (6)29 (7)17
(8)38 (9)48 (10)50 (11)8 (12)65 (13)50
(14)7 (15)36 (16)3 (17)57 (18)15 (19)30
(20)7 (21)36 (22)59 (23)46 (24)43 (25)26
(26)7 (27)8 (28)24 (29)32 (30)33

Page 40, Item 1:
(1)49 (2)4 (3)21 (4)15 (5)1 (6)1 (7)26 (8)69
(9)47 (10)13 (11)30 (12)78 (13)25 (14)50
(15)2 (16)3 (17)14 (18)0 (19)49 (20)35
(21)54 (22)29 (23)11 (24)17 (25)67 (26)5
(27)19 (28)18 (29)1 (30)24

Page 42, Item 1:
(1)12 (2)18 (3)50 (4)45 (5)14 (6)21 (7)12
(8)18 (9)6 (10)28 (11)28 (12)6 (13)3 (14)8
(15)3 (16)20 (17)36 (18)20 (19)5 (20)1
(21)25 (22)24 (23)12 (24)10 (25)50 (26)24
(27)9 (28)9 (29)6 (30)30

Page 43, Item 1:
(1)4 (2)16 (3)3 (4)36 (5)25 (6)20 (7)8 (8)4
(9)4 (10)15 (11)4 (12)10 (13)12 (14)18
(15)18 (16)2 (17)40 (18)3 (19)12 (20)35
(21)15 (22)4 (23)16 (24)2 (25)2 (26)5
(27)45 (28)2 (29)2 (30)30

Page 44, Item 1:
(1)15 (2)20 (3)40 (4)15 (5)30 (6)35 (7)10
(8)40 (9)6 (10)40 (11)16 (12)6 (13)3
(14)30 (15)5 (16)20 (17)6 (18)5 (19)2
(20)40 (21)50 (22)28 (23)20 (24)1 (25)35
(26)4 (27)36 (28)45 (29)45 (30)40

Page 45, Item 1:
(1)18 (2)8 (3)28 (4)27 (5)27 (6)24 (7)8 (8)1
(9)24 (10)10 (11)5 (12)15 (13)24 (14)12
(15)14 (16)27 (17)40 (18)25 (19)8 (20)12
(21)20 (22)7 (23)6 (24)15 (25)36 (26)20
(27)8 (28)12 (29)16 (30)28

Page 46, Item 1:
(1)28 (2)10 (3)15 (4)4 (5)5 (6)3 (7)14 (8)12
(9)8 (10)8 (11)40 (12)4 (13)2 (14)2 (15)12
(16)12 (17)3 (18)14 (19)10 (20)15 (21)3
(22)50 (23)2 (24)3 (25)12 (26)20 (27)27
(28)15 (29)10 (30)32

Page 47, Item 1:
(1)35 (2)45 (3)24 (4)45 (5)4 (6)45 (7)15

(8)18 (9)24 (10)4 (11)9 (12)10 (13)20
(14)6 (15)6 (16)5 (17)14 (18)4 (19)1 (20)7
(21)15 (22)12 (23)30 (24)50 (25)6 (26)4
(27)18 (28)21 (29)30 (30)2

Page 48, Item 1:
(1)8 (2)8 (3)6 (4)45 (5)35 (6)20 (7)8 (8)20
(9)3 (10)14 (11)40 (12)30 (13)24 (14)15
(15)20 (16)21 (17)16 (18)2 (19)30 (20)28
(21)14 (22)15 (23)10 (24)28 (25)36 (26)16
(27)9 (28)4 (29)6 (30)4

Page 49, Item 1:
(1)3 (2)10 (3)15 (4)28 (5)18 (6)20 (7)20
(8)8 (9)18 (10)2 (11)40 (12)18 (13)30
(14)24 (15)20 (16)20 (17)40 (18)12 (19)36
(20)12 (21)14 (22)20 (23)7 (24)45 (25)10
(26)1 (27)40 (28)2 (29)4 (30)30

Page 51, Item 1:
(1)50 (2)32 (3)24 (4)49 (5)12 (6)27 (7)63
(8)60 (9)42 (10)40 (11)90 (12)8 (13)60
(14)40 (15)54 (16)9 (17)12 (18)40 (19)30
(20)8 (21)7 (22)70 (23)42 (24)21 (25)80
(26)72 (27)54 (28)56 (29)100 (30)32

Page 52, Item 1:
(1)35 (2)16 (3)18 (4)24 (5)30 (6)45 (7)48
(8)70 (9)18 (10)18 (11)70 (12)64 (13)48
(14)30 (15)56 (16)81 (17)60 (18)20 (19)28
(20)24 (21)54 (22)63 (23)56 (24)63 (25)54
(26)7 (27)40 (28)14 (29)48 (30)40

Page 53, Item 1:

(1)40 (2)60 (3)20 (4)48 (5)64 (6)72 (7)70
(8)42 (9)56 (10)7 (11)28 (12)28 (13)49
(14)18 (15)81 (16)70 (17)70 (18)70 (19)32
(20)100 (21)80 (22)70 (23)36 (24)6 (25)28
(26)35 (27)7 (28)56 (29)28 (30)30

Page 54, Item 1:

(1)70 (2)56 (3)24 (4)54 (5)100 (6)48 (7)21
(8)24 (9)6 (10)100 (11)7 (12)49 (13)42
(14)63 (15)50 (16)6 (17)9 (18)32 (19)35
(20)63 (21)56 (22)24 (23)70 (24)9 (25)35
(26)35 (27)63 (28)54 (29)36 (30)20

Page 55, Item 1:

(1)63 (2)27 (3)24 (4)60 (5)72 (6)32 (7)72
(8)16 (9)28 (10)28 (11)16 (12)8 (13)80
(14)9 (15)8 (16)54 (17)12 (18)48 (19)90
(20)72 (21)7 (22)21 (23)90 (24)7 (25)90
(26)40 (27)8 (28)24 (29)7 (30)54

Page 56, Item 1:

(1)18 (2)40 (3)40 (4)21 (5)30 (6)18 (7)72
(8)42 (9)64 (10)50 (11)12 (12)49 (13)80
(14)27 (15)80 (16)8 (17)48 (18)32 (19)49
(20)21 (21)63 (22)42 (23)54 (24)54 (25)56
(26)18 (27)80 (28)42 (29)42 (30)70

Page 57, Item 1:

(1)35 (2)6 (3)24 (4)48 (5)54 (6)56 (7)36
(8)27 (9)8 (10)56 (11)72 (12)32 (13)21
(14)70 (15)42 (16)10 (17)60 (18)70 (19)70
(20)24 (21)14 (22)80 (23)60 (24)24 (25)80
(26)8 (27)56 (28)24 (29)24 (30)18

Page 58, Item 1:

(1)14 (2)32 (3)36 (4)72 (5)36 (6)21 (7)60
(8)63 (9)45 (10)54 (11)21 (12)48 (13)100
(14)32 (15)54 (16)54 (17)42 (18)56 (19)40
(20)30 (21)81 (22)56 (23)54 (24)10 (25)28
(26)28 (27)48 (28)12 (29)30 (30)70

Page 60, Item 1:

(1)D (2)D (3)B (4)D (5)A (6)B (7)D (8)A (9)D

Page 61, Item 1:

(1)B (2)D (3)C (4)A (5)C (6)B (7)C (8)C (9)B

Page 62, Item 1:

(1)C (2)A (3)D (4)B (5)B (6)A (7)C (8)A (9)D

Page 63, Item 1:

(1)D (2)A (3)D (4)D (5)D (6)D (7)C (8)A (9)C

Page 64, Item 1:

(1)D (2)B (3)D (4)A (5)A (6)A (7)C (8)B (9)C

Page 65, Item 1:

(1)D (2)A (3)C (4)A (5)A (6)B (7)B (8)C (9)B

Page 66, Item 1:

(1)A (2)C (3)C (4)A (5)C (6)A (7)C (8)C (9)B

Page 67, Item 1:

(1)A (2)C (3)C (4)A (5)A (6)C (7)C (8)A (9)D

Page 69, Item 1:

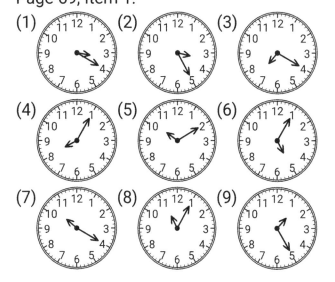

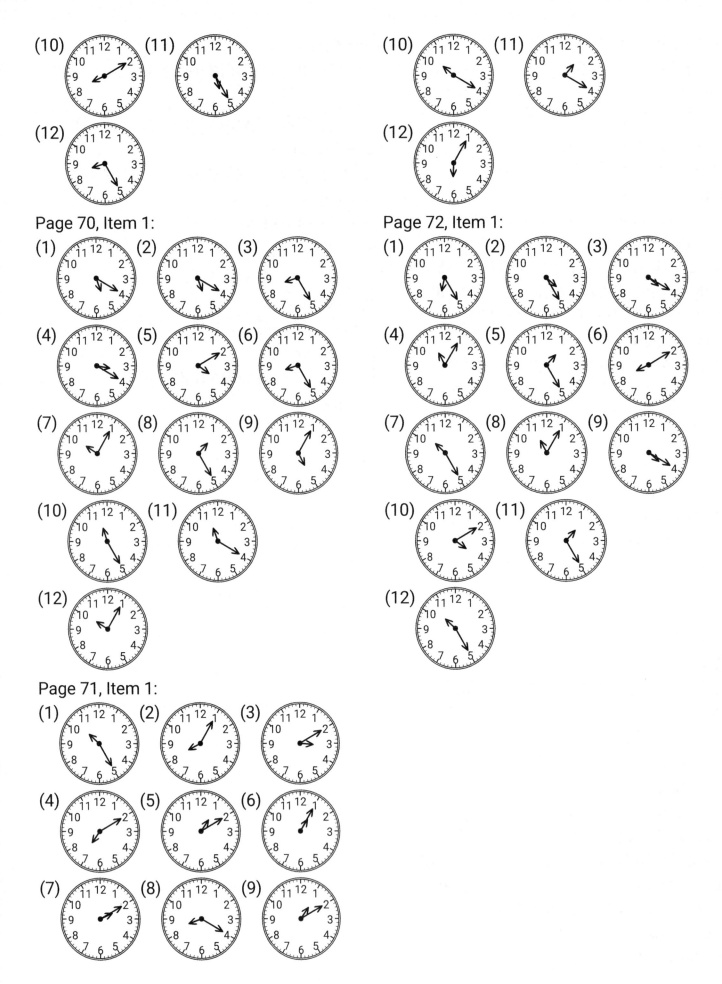

(10) (11)

(12)

(10) (11)

(12)

Page 70, Item 1:

(1) (2) (3)

(4) (5) (6)

(7) (8) (9)

(10) (11)

(12)

Page 72, Item 1:

(1) (2) (3)

(4) (5) (6)

(7) (8) (9)

(10) (11)

(12)

Page 71, Item 1:

(1) (2) (3)

(4) (5) (6)

(7) (8) (9)

Page 73, Item 1:

(1) (2) (3)
(4) (5) (6)
(7) (8) (9)
(10) (11)
(12)

Page 75, Item 1:

(1) (2) (3)
(4) (5) (6)
(7) (8) (9)
(10) (11)
(12)

Page 74, Item 1:

(1) (2) (3)
(4) (5) (6)
(7) (8) (9)
(10) (11)
(12)

Page 76, Item 1:

(1) (2) (3)
(4) (5) (6)

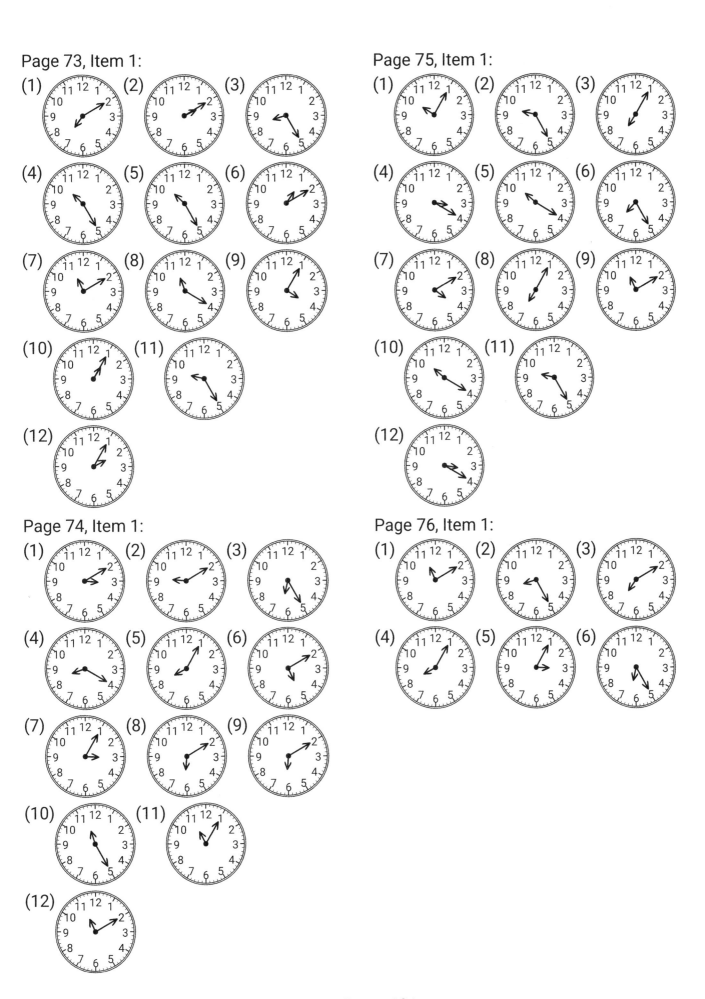

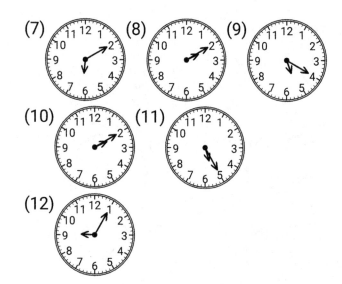

(7)

(8)

(9)

(10)

(11)

(12)

Page 78, Item 1:
(1)4/5 (2)3/4 (3)1/10 (4)2/8 (5)2/9 (6)3/7
(7)4/6 (8)1/10 (9)3/8 (10)2/9 (11)1/4
(12)1/6 (13)1/5 (14)4/7 (15)3/8 (16)2/10
(17)1/7 (18)3/9 (19)4/6 (20)2/4 (21)4/5

Page 79, Item 1:
(1)1/7 (2)4/8 (3)2/5 (4)3/10 (5)4/6 (6)3/9
(7)2/4 (8)1/5 (9)1/4 (10)2/9 (11)4/7
(12)3/10 (13)2/6 (14)4/8 (15)1/10 (16)3/9
(17)2/6 (18)4/5 (19)1/4 (20)3/7 (21)4/8

Page 80, Item 1:
(1)3/4 (2)4/9 (3)2/10 (4)1/7 (5)2/8 (6)3/6
(7)4/5 (8)1/7 (9)1/4 (10)1/8 (11)3/5
(12)2/6 (13)3/9 (14)4/10 (15)1/10 (16)2/5
(17)3/4 (18)1/6 (19)4/8 (20)2/9 (21)1/7

Page 81, Item 1:
(1)4/7 (2)2/6 (3)3/8 (4)1/5 (5)1/9 (6)2/10
(7)3/4 (8)1/4 (9)1/8 (10)3/6 (11)2/9
(12)4/5 (13)3/7 (14)1/10 (15)4/9 (16)2/5
(17)4/10 (18)2/8 (19)3/6 (20)1/4 (21)2/7

Page 82, Item 1:
(1)4/5 (2)3/4 (3)2/6 (4)1/9 (5)3/7 (6)4/8
(7)1/10 (8)2/6 (9)2/8 (10)3/10 (11)1/4
(12)1/9 (13)3/5 (14)1/7 (15)2/5 (16)4/10
(17)3/4 (18)4/7 (19)1/8 (20)2/9 (21)4/6

Page 83, Item 1:
(1)3/5 (2)2/6 (3)4/7 (4)1/4 (5)2/9 (6)4/8
(7)3/10 (8)1/10 (9)3/4 (10)4/8 (11)1/7
(12)2/6 (13)4/5 (14)3/9 (15)1/7 (16)2/9
(17)1/6 (18)3/10 (19)1/4 (20)2/5 (21)2/8

Page 84, Item 1:
(1)1/4 (2)1/8 (3)2/9 (4)3/7 (5)3/5 (6)4/6
(7)1/10 (8)2/7 (9)3/4 (10)1/6 (11)4/8
(12)2/10 (13)2/5 (14)3/9 (15)1/8 (16)4/5
(17)4/6 (18)2/9 (19)3/7 (20)1/10 (21)3/4

Page 86, Item 1:
(1)3/4 (2)4/5 (3)1/8 (4)1/3 (5)5/7 (6)2/6
(7)1/2 (8)2/3 (9)4/6 (10)2/2 (11)2/7

(12)2/5

Page 87, Item 1:
(1)2/5 (2)3/6 (3)1/2 (4)3/3 (5)4/4 (6)6/8
(7)1/7 (8)3/7 (9)3/4 (10)4/8 (11)1/3
(12)3/6

Page 88, Item 1:
(1)1/4 (2)1/3 (3)1/5 (4)1/2 (5)1/7 (6)3/6
(7)1/8 (8)2/5 (9)2/6 (10)3/3 (11)5/7
(12)2/8

Page 89, Item 1:
(1)2/6 (2)1/8 (3)4/5 (4)1/2 (5)3/3 (6)1/7
(7)3/4 (8)3/5 (9)4/4 (10)3/7 (11)6/8
(12)1/2

Page 90, Item 1:
(1)2/5 (2)2/4 (3)1/2 (4)7/8 (5)2/3 (6)5/6
(7)1/7 (8)3/4 (9)1/2 (10)5/7 (11)4/6
(12)2/3

Page 91, Item 1:
(1)6/7 (2)4/8 (3)3/3 (4)2/2 (5)2/4 (6)1/5
(7)2/6 (8)1/5 (9)1/7 (10)7/8 (11)1/3
(12)1/4

Page 92, Item 1:
(1)3/7 (2)2/5 (3)2/3 (4)5/6 (5)1/8 (6)1/4
(7)2/2 (8)2/3 (9)1/4 (10)3/8 (11)2/7
(12)2/5

Made in the USA
Columbia, SC
09 July 2025

60538245R00057